To _____

_____

_____

From _____

_____

_____

Date _____

_____

Recipes created and compiled by Colleen Miner, Twin Cities cooking instructor, TV personality, and certified member of the International Association of Culinary Professionals (IACP).

The rest of the material has been collected over an extended period of time. The original authors are unknown, so regretfully credit may not be attributed to the original authors.

TREAT YOURSELF™ is a collection of quick and easy culinary pleasures and whimsical thoughts for each day of the year. Each recipe is an opportunity for you, the reader, to take a moment to be good to yourself and those you cook for – even young children can prepare many of these fun delights!

Cover design – Marcia Carlson
Additional material compiled by Victoria Lesman Estrem

FOR FOOD, FOR FRIENDS, FOR FELLOWSHIP AND FOR YOU

May this food to be prepared
Be blessed with love and tender care.
May those who feast upon these treats
Be blessed with happiness as they eat.
Bless family, friends, but above all else
Don't forget to bless – and

TREAT YOURSELF

HOW TO MELT CHOCOLATE OR CANDY COATING

This process is trickier than it may seem. Chocolate and coating are sensitive to heat and moisture.

Two ways to melt are:

1. Place chocolate or coating in double boiler over hot, but *NOT* boiling water. Stir until melted.

2. Place chocolate or coating in microwave glass bowl on 30% power for 2 minute intervals until melted.

DIETER'S DELITE CHOCOLATE SAUCE

3 T. unsweetened
   cocoa powder
1½ tsp. cornstarch
1½ tsp. sugar

3 T. skim milk
1/3 c. corn syrup
1/2 tsp. vanilla

Sift cocoa, cornstarch and sugar in a pan. Gradually add milk and corn syrup. Bring to a boil, stirring constantly. Reduce heat and simmer for 2 minutes. Whisk in vanilla. Cool and use over fruit or frozen yogurt.

Yesterday is experience, tomorrow is hope, today is getting from one to the other.

JANUARY 1

TORTELLINI KABOBS

1 package fresh cheese tortellini
1 package fresh cheese spinach tortellini
Pimento
Picante sauce

Cook tortellini according to package instructions, rinse with cold water and drain. Skewer a white tortellini, a pimento and a green tortellini. Serve with picante sauce.

*You'll never strain your eyes by looking at
the bright side of things.*

DECEMBER 31

COCOA MERINGUES

1/4 c. cocoa powder
3 egg whites
1/8 tsp. cream of tartar
1/2 c. sugar

Beat egg whites in a large bowl with an electric mixer on low speed until frothy. Add cream of tartar and beat on high speed until soft peaks form. Add sugar one tablespoon at a time. Fold in the cocoa and beat until incorporated. Drop by spoonful onto parchment lined cookie sheet. Bake for 1½ hours at 225°. Turn off oven and let cool in oven with the door closed for two hours.

JANUARY 2

ARTICHOKE PUFFS

3/4 c. cheddar cheese, grated
1/2 c. mayonnaise
1/2 tsp. onion salt

1 can artichoke hearts,
drained and cut into
quarters
30 melba rounds

Add first three ingredients. Place one piece of artichoke heart on the melba round. Top each canapé with a spoonful of the mixture. Place under broiler until the cheese puffs.

There's a new toy designed to help a child adjust to today's world – any way it's put together, it's wrong.

DECEMBER 30

ORANGE HONEY BUTTER

1 stick butter, at room temperature
2 T. honey
2 tsp. orange juice
2 T. grated orange rind

Beat butter until smooth. Add honey, orange juice, and orange rind. Mix until blended.

Two things a person should never be angry at: what they can help, and what they can't.

JANUARY 3

PERSIMMON SLUSH

Persimmon

Place ripe persimmon in the freezer. When it is frozen, cut off top and scoop out pulp with spoon and eat.

Beware of those who like to have their cake – and yours too.

DECEMBER 29

ORANGE PECAN POPOVERS

1 popover mix, prepared
1/8 c. pecans, finely chopped
1 tsp. grated orange rind

To prepared mix, add pecans and the orange rind. Blend, but do not over beat. Pour batter into buttered custard cups or muffin tin. Bake at 425° for 30 minutes.

The only food that doesn't go up in price is food for thought.

JANUARY 4

CLAM DIP

8 oz. package cream cheese
1 can minced clams, drained
2 green onions, chopped
1 T. Worcestershire sauce

Combine all ingredients and serve with chips and vegetables for dipping.

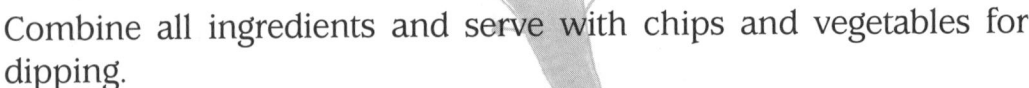

*Keeping a tight lip pays off when you are angry
and when the hors d'oeuvres tray is passed.*

DECEMBER 28

STRAWBERRY SAUCE

1 package frozen strawberries, thawed
1 T. lemon juice

Puree all ingredients in a blender. Cover and refrigerate. Use with fruit or ice cream.

If you can tell the difference between good advice and bad advice you don't need advice.

JANUARY 5

STAR PANCAKES

Pancake batter
2 T. butter
Powdered sugar

Heat pan with butter. Place pancake batter in a pitcher. Pour batter into pan slowly making a star pattern. Flip once. Remove from pan and sprinkle with powdered sugar.

Children have plenty of will power –
but even more won't power.

DECEMBER 27

ROLL UP REUBEN

1 loaf of white bread dough, thawed
1 c. Swiss cheese, shredded
6 oz. corned beef
1 c. sauerkraut, drained and patted dry

Roll out thawed bread dough to a 12 by 10 inch rectangle. Cover dough with corned beef to within 1/2 inch of the edge, then spread on cheese and sauerkraut. Roll up jelly roll fashion along the long side. Place seam side down on a baking sheet. Cover and let rise for 30 minutes. Bake at 375° for 20 minutes. Slice and serve.

Never pick a quarrel even when it's ripe.

JANUARY 6

ONION, BLUE CHEESE, WALNUT PIZZA

2 onions, thinly sliced
2 T. butter
1/2 c. blue cheese, crumbled
1/2 c. walnuts, toasted
1 precooked pizza crust

Melt butter in pan and cook the onions slowly, stirring occasionally, until soft and golden. Spread over pizza crust, sprinkle with cheese and nuts. Bake at 450° for 10 minutes.

To be rich is no longer a sin, it's a miracle.

DECEMBER 26

CHERRY YOGURT SHAKE

1/2 c. canned bing cherries, drained
2 T. honey
1 c. vanilla yogurt
2 ice cubes

Puree cherries in a blender. Add honey, yogurt and ice cubes. Process at high speed until frothy. Serve immediately.

Enjoy yourself! These are the good old days you are going to miss in ten years.

JANUARY 7

Eggnog French Toast

6 slices of raisin bread
2 c. eggnog
2 T. butter
Powdered sugar

Dip raisin bread in the egg nog. Heat butter in a pan until hot. Sauté the bread in the pan turning once until golden brown. Remove and sprinkle with powdered sugar.

The best gifts in life are tied with your heartstrings.

DECEMBER 25

Peanut Butter and Jelly Pocket Sandwiches

1 roll refrigerated biscuit dough
8 tsp. peanut butter
8 tsp. jelly, your favorite flavor

Flatten each biscuit on a greased pan. Top each biscuit with 1 tsp. each of peanut butter and jelly. Fold over and seal edges. Bake according to the directions on the package.

Definition of a silly game: one your child can beat you at.

JANUARY 8

SWEET ROLL TREE

2 rolls refrigerated cinnamon roll dough
Green sugar
Red cinnamon candies

Arrange rolls on a cookie sheet in a tree shape, starting with one, then two, then three and so on. Use a roll for the tree trunk. Bake according to package instructions. Frost and sprinkle with green and red cinnamon candies.

Live your hopes, not your desires.

DECEMBER 24

BAGEL CHIPS

1 bagel
1 T. oil
1 T. parmesan cheese
1 tsp garlic salt

Slice bagel into thin circles. Brush lightly with oil. Sprinkle on parmesan cheese and garlic salt. Bake at 325° for 10 minutes.

The only thing some people know how to cook is your goose.

JANUARY 9

EDIBLE PAINT FOR SUGAR COOKIES

2 egg yolks
1/2 T. of 4 assorted food coloring

Beat yolks in a small dish and divide among 4 custard cups. Stir 1/2 T. of coloring into each cup. Paint uncooked sugar cookie dough and bake.

Christmas toys are educational – they teach children that their parents will buy almost anything.

DECEMBER 23

Winter Jelly

1 c. water
3¼ c. sugar
3 T. lemon juice
1 pouch liquid pectin
3/4 c. pineapple orange juice concentrate, thawed

Combine sugar and water in a large pot. Place on high heat and, stirring constantly, bring to a boil. Add lemon juice and boil for 1 minute. Remove from heat, add pectin and juice concentrate, mix well. Ladle into sterilized jars and seal.

Jelly is the stuff you see on toast, neckties, and piano keys.

JANUARY 10

STAINED GLASS WINDOW COOKIES

1 roll refrigerated sugar cookie dough
Hard candy, assorted colors
Aluminum foil

Take 1/4 c. of the dough and roll it into snakes. Place the dough on the foil resembling a stained glass window. Crush the candies with a rolling pin or processor, keeping the colors separate. Place a spoonful of different color crushed candy in each window pane. Bake in a 375° oven for 8 minutes. Let completely cool on foil and peel off.

The best gift is a family that is all wrapped up in each other.

DECEMBER 22

PURPLE COW

1 c. ice cream
1/4 c. milk
3 T. frozen grape juice concentrate

Combine ice cream, milk, and frozen juice concentrate in a blender.
Cover and blend until smooth. Serve immediately.

Make the most of yourself, for that is all there is of you.

JANUARY 11

CINNAMON ORNAMENTS

A treat for the nose, NOT the mouth!

1 c. cinnamon   3/4 c. apple sauce

Mix the cinnamon and apple sauce together and microwave till warm. Roll out mixture like cookie dough in a flour cinnamon mixture. Cut out ornaments with cookie cutters, being sure to make a hole for hanging. Dry until hard. Flip every 24 hours for 3-4 days.

A healthy diet is easier to follow if you have kids around the house to consume the junk food.

DECEMBER 21

ROASTED BANANA

1 banana, very ripe
1/8 tsp. butter

Remove a thin strip of peel, and brush the exposed banana with butter. Roast in a 400° oven for 10 minutes. Eat directly from the peel with a spoon.

*There's no sense in advertising your troubles –
there's no market for them.*

JANUARY 12

MARZIPAN

8 oz. almond paste   Food coloring
3 T. light corn syrup   1/2 c. superfine sugar
1 c. confectioner sugar

Knead paste to soften by hand. Continue kneading and add corn syrup 1 T. at a time. Stir in confectioner sugar. Separate dough and add food coloring. Shape into a variety of fruits and vegetables. Roll in superfine sugar.

*If nothing else, winter gives us plenty of reasons
to look forward to spring.*

DECEMBER 20

LOW CAL FRENCH FRIES

2 potatoes, scrubbed
Vegetable oil spray
Salt

Cut each potato into 8 wedges. Spray the wedges generously with vegetable spray and sprinkle with salt. Bake at 400° for 30 minutes, turning once.

*Those who say they are going on a diet
are just wishful shrinkers.*

JANUARY 13

POACHED ORANGES

6 large navel oranges, peeled and sliced
1 c. red wine
1/4 c. sugar
1 cinnamon stick

Place the wine, sugar, and cinnamon stick in a pan and bring it to a boil. Boil for 5 minutes and remove from heat. Add sliced oranges and let cool.

No matter how hard they try to reduce,
some people are never a bargain.

DECEMBER 19

FILLED WON TON COOKIES

1/2 c. salted peanuts, chopped
1/2 c. coconut
1/2 c. brown sugar

Won ton wrappers
Cooking oil
Powdered sugar

Mix together nuts, coconut and brown sugar. Fold won ton squares into triangles and round off corners with a scissors. Unfold and place 2 tsp. of the filling in center. Moisten edges with water and refold. Cook in hot oil until golden, turning once. Drain on paper towel and sprinkle with powdered sugar.

Success lies upstream, you can't just drift there.

JANUARY 14

CANDIED ORANGE PEEL

1 large navel orange   1/4 c. sugar
1/4 c. water   2 T. sugar, for coating

Peel orange, removing just the colored part of the rind. Cut into match stick strips. Place in a pan with cold water and bring to a boil. Boil for 5 minutes. Rinse peel and return to pan with 1/4 c. sugar and 1/4 c. water. Bring to boil, reduce heat and simmer for 25 minutes. Drain and roll in sugar. Leave on a rack to dry.

*Temper is one of the few things that improves
when you don't use it.*

DECEMBER 18

APPLE TREATS

1 apple
4 T. cream cheese
1 T. raisins

Mix cream cheese and raisins. Core apple and stuff with cream cheese mixture. Slice apple or eat whole.

Adam and Eve living in the Garden of Eden couldn't complain how much better things were in the good old days.

JANUARY 15

SUGARED NUTS

4 T. butter, melted
1 lb. pecan halves
1 1/3 c. sugar

1 tsp. cinnamon
2 egg whites

Pour butter over nuts in a bowl, then sprinkle the sugar and cinnamon over the nuts. Beat egg whites to soft peaks and gradually add sugar. Fold nuts into egg whites and spread out on baking sheet. Bake for 25 minutes, stirring every 10 minutes.

Holiday time is when a lot of people come unglued trying to wrap things up.

DECEMBER 17

BREAKFAST PASTA

1 egg
4 oz. of spaghetti
1 tsp. butter
1/4 c. grated cheese

Cook pasta in boiling water until tender. Drain and return to the pan. Beat egg and pour over hot pasta along with butter and cheese. Place over low heat and stir until egg is set on the pasta and cheese is melted.

Early to bed and early to rise makes a man get his own breakfast.

JANUARY 16

EGGLESS NOG

1 pint frozen low-fat vanilla yogurt
1 c. low fat milk
1/2 tsp. vanilla
1/2 tsp. ground nutmeg

Whirl all ingredients in a blender and serve chilled.

A sweater is something you put on a child when you're cold.

DECEMBER 16

STUFFED CUCUMBER SLICES

1 large cucumber
3 oz. cream cheese and chives
1 T. blue cheese

Score cucumber with a fork lengthwise over the entire surface. Cut a 1 inch slice from each end and hollow out cucumber with a spoon. Fill hollow with cream cheese that has been mixed with blue cheese. Wrap in foil and refrigerate for 3 hours. Slice and serve.

*If you don't grow your own vegetables,
praise your neighbor's garden.*

JANUARY 17

POLAR HOT CHOCOLATE

1 cup of your favorite hot chocolate
1 peppermint stick

Stir chocolate with the peppermint stick. Bite off the tip and sip the hot chocolate through it like a straw.

*Holiday time is when we get children
something for their parents to play with.*

DECEMBER 15

Golden Raisin Truffles

1/2 c. golden raisins, coarsely chopped
10 oz. white chocolate, chopped fine
1/3 c. cream
Powdered sugar

Melt chocolate with cream. Add raisins. Cover and refrigerate until set, about 4 hours. Scoop into balls and roll in powdered sugar.

Happiness is the best of all riches – and it's not taxed.

JANUARY 18

Chocolate Chip Pancakes

2 c. pancake mix, prepared according to instructions
1 c. chocolate chips

Add chocolate chips to prepared pancake mix. Fry in hot, greased pan until bubbles form on surface, then turn and brown on the other side.

A family unit is not only composed of children, but of men, women, an occasional animal and the common cold.

DECEMBER 14

CHOCOLATE PEANUT BUTTER POPS

20 Ritz® crackers
1/4 c. peanut butter
10 popsicle sticks
6 oz. chocolate chips

Spread about 1/2 T. peanut butter on a cracker. Press the stick into place and top with another cracker. Melt the chocolate chips and dip the crackers into it. Place on wax paper to set.

Family – the thing most needed in the American home today.

JANUARY 19

MERINGUE DROPS

2 egg whites   1/2 c. sugar
1/2 tsp. cream of tartar   1/4 tsp. vanilla

Beat egg whites slowly until they foam. Add cream of tartar and beat on high speed. Add sugar gradually and then beat in vanilla. Drop the meringue by the spoonful on a cookie sheet lined with parchment paper. Bake in a 200° oven for 2 hours. Then turn off heat and leave meringues in oven for another hour.

Happiness is a place between too much and too little.

DECEMBER 13

CHOCOLATE BANANA SHAKE

1/2 banana
1/2 c. skim milk
2 T. chocolate syrup
4 ice cubes

Combine banana, skim milk, and chocolate syrup in blender and process on high speed. Add ice cubes one at a time with the blender running. Serve frothy.

Nothing you put in a banana split is as fattening as the spoon.

JANUARY 20

EGGNOG FONDUE

3 oz. package vanilla pudding
2 c. eggnog

Heat eggnog and pudding mix in a pan according to package instructions. Serve warm with fruit and pound cake for dipping.

He who laughs, lasts.

DECEMBER 12

TORTILLA BREAKFAST STICKS

4 flour tortillas
2 oz. cream cheese
1/4 c. raspberry jam

Cut tortilla in half. Divide jam and cream cheese among the 8 tortilla halves. Roll tortilla and bake seam side down at 350° for 10 minutes.

Real friends are those who, when you've made a fool of yourself, don't feel that you have done a permanent job.

JANUARY 21

POPCORN TREES

Prepared vanilla frosting, dyed green
6 sugar cones
3 cups popped corn
Red cinnamon candies

Spread the frosting on the outside of the cone to cover, press popped corn into the frosting. Dot with red candies.

*To err is human, but to really foul things up
requires a computer.*

DECEMBER 11

Mary's Veggie Squares

1 package refrigerated crescent roll dough
8 oz. cream cheese
1 c. sour cream
1 package powdered ranch dressing mix
3 c. chopped raw vegetables – carrots, peppers, scallions, etc.

Press whole sheet of crescent roll dough into pan. Bake according to instructions. When crust is cool, spread with a mixture of cream cheese, sour cream and dressing mix. Sprinkle vegetables over crust and cut into squares. Serve chilled.

JANUARY 22

SNOWBALLS

1 pint peppermint ice cream, or flavor of your choice
1 c. shredded coconut

Scoop ice cream into balls and roll in coconut. Wrap in plastic wrap and freeze.

One good turn gets most of the blanket.

DECEMBER 10

SURPRISE ANGEL FOOD

1 loaf angel food cake
1 pint raspberry sherbet, softened
Chocolate syrup

Cut off 1/2 inch slice off the top of the cake. Cut a 1/2 inch border around loaf. Scoop out the interior and fill hole with softened sherbet. Replace top and press in place. Freeze until ready to serve. Top with chocolate sauce.

The design on a birthday cake is often beautiful, but the arithmetic is usually terrible.

JANUARY 23

CHOCOLATE SPOONS

1/2 c. milk chocolate, chopped   Plastic spoons, red and green

Melt chocolate. Prop spoons so that bowls are level. Place chocolate in a plastic bag and cut a small hole in the corner. Pipe chocolate into each spoon bowl. Let chocolate harden and individually wrap spoons in plastic wrap tied with a ribbon. Remove wrapper and stir into a cup of coffee.

Christmas is when we wish people didn't come in different sizes.

DECEMBER 9

BLUE CHEESE BISCUITS

1 package refrigerated biscuit dough
2 T. margarine, melted
3 T. blue cheese, crumbled

Cut biscuits into bite size pieces. Place in pan and drizzle with margarine and sprinkle with cheese. Bake in a 400° oven for 15 minutes.

Some people go anywhere for dinner – except the kitchen.

JANUARY 24

EGGS IN A CLOUD

2 eggs

Carefully separate the eggs. Whip the whites until stiff. Spray two custard dishes with vegetable spray and put 1/2 the egg whites in each dish. Make a small depression in each dish and slip egg yolk into it. Bake in a 350° oven for 10 minutes.

Breakfast in bed is the hardest meal for a mother to get.

DECEMBER 8

CARAMEL TRUFFLES

8 oz. milk chocolate, chopped
4 T. butter
1/3 c. caramel topping
1 c. pecans, chopped

Melt chocolate with the butter. Beat in caramel. Chill until firm and roll in chopped pecans.

*Don't worry about avoiding temptation –
as you grow older it starts avoiding you.*

JANUARY 25

MINT BARK

1 lb. vanilla coating, finely chopped
3/4 c. peppermint candy, crushed

Melt the coating in a glass bowl in a microwave oven for 3 minutes at 30% power or until melted. Add peppermint candy and blend. Pour onto aluminum foil covered pan. Spread to about a 1/2 inch thickness. Chill until firm, then break into pieces.

*The food that is put into the mind must be watched
as closely as the food that's put into the body.*

DECEMBER 7

APRICOT TODDY

6 oz. apricot nectar
1 T. sugar
1 T. lemon juice
Stick of cinnamon

Heat all ingredients together and serve.

*It's not always best to do unto others as you would have
them do unto you – your tastes may be different.*

JANUARY 26

Rosy Wine Jelly

2 c. rosé wine
3 c. sugar
3 oz. package of liquid pectin

Combine wine and sugar in saucepan and bring to boil over medium heat stirring frequently. Add pectin and return to a boil, stirring, for 1 minute. Pour into a sterilized wine glass and seal with melted paraffin.

*You aren't really old until you're glad
to see another birthday.*

DECEMBER 6

HOT PEPPER RICE CAKE

4 rice cakes
4 T. cream cheese
4 T. hot pepper jelly

Spread rice cakes with cream cheese and top with pepper jelly.

*Even though we all live under the same sky, it is interesting
how many horizons there are.*

JANUARY 27

CRISPY SNOWFLAKES

10 - 8 inch tortillas
1/2 c. peanut oil
Powdered sugar

Wrap tortillas in foil and heat in 325° oven for 10 minutes. Fold in half and in quarter. Cut pattern out with a scissors as you would a snowflake. Fry one tortilla at a time in oil until light brown, turning once. Drain and sprinkle with powdered sugar.

I do not object to the snow falling, I object to me falling.

DECEMBER 5

OATMEAL CRISPS COOKIES

2 c. regular rolled oats
1 c. brown sugar
2 tsp. baking powder
1 stick butter, melted
1 egg, beaten

Mix the oats, sugar and baking powder together. Add butter to the mixture, then stir in the beaten egg. Drop dough onto parchment lined cookie sheet. Bake at 350° for 10 minutes. Let cool a minute and remove from cookie sheet.

When things go wrong, don't go with them.

JANUARY 28

GUMDROP TULIPS

Gumdrops, variety of colors

Cut gumdrop from top down in "x" formation cutting almost to the bottom. Separate the sections slightly. Place a different colored gumdrop slice in the center.

A family is a group of people, no two of whom like the same ingredient on a pizza.

DECEMBER 4

ASIAN CHICKEN WINGS

1/2 c. soy sauce
1/3 c. sugar
3 T. sesame oil
3 T. dry sherry
1/4 c. sesame seeds
2 lb. chicken wings

Marinate chicken wings in a mixture of the other ingredients for 1 hour.
Place in 350° oven until golden, about 40 minutes.

Advice to after-dinner speakers:
Be honest, be direct, be seated.

JANUARY 29

SCOTTISH SHORTBREAD

1¼ c. flour   1 stick butter
1/4 c. confectioner sugar   1 tsp. vanilla

Stir together the flour and sugar, then cut in the butter. Add the vanilla and blend. Knead into a smooth ball and pat into an 8 inch circle on an ungreased cookie sheet. Prick with a fork and cut dough into 12 wedges, but do not separate. Bake at 325° for 25 minutes.

Time may be a great healer, but it's a lousy beautician.

DECEMBER 3

PESTO BREAD

Loaf of French bread, sliced
1/4 c. butter
4 oz. jar of pesto
1/4 c. parmesan cheese

Spread butter on bread. Top with pesto and sprinkle with parmesan cheese. Place slices on cookie sheet and broil for 3 minutes until cheese melts.

Never let the opportunity to say a kind word pass.

JANUARY 30

"BACON AND EGGS"

1 c. white candy coating, chopped and melted
Yellow M&M's
Small stick pretzels

Carefully melt the chopped candy. Line a cookie sheet with wax paper and drop a teaspoon of bark on the wax paper, top with a yellow M&M and two pretzel sticks side by side creating the effect of "bacon and eggs".

More often than not these days the chip is considerably bigger than the old block.

DECEMBER 2

Tutti Frutti Ice Cream

1 quart vanilla ice cream, softened
1 c. stale fruit cake, finely chopped

Mix chopped fruit cake into ice cream and place in freezer until firm.

Happiness is having a scratch for every itch.

JANUARY 31

Brie Melt

1 small brie wheel
1/4 c. chopped pecans
1/4 c. brown sugar

Take the top off the brie wheel and discard. Press the pecan and brown sugar combination into the top of the brie. Bake at 350° for 5 minutes.

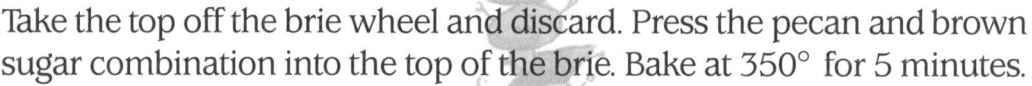

Christmas is the time when you buy this year's gifts with next year's money.

DECEMBER 1

CINNAMON CIDER

1 c. apple cider
1 T. red cinnamon candy

Combine cider and cinnamon candy in a saucepan and heat until the candy melts. Serve warm in a mug.

Most of the shadows of this life are caused by standing in your own sunshine.

FEBRUARY 1

Hot Apple Toddy

1 c. apple cider
1 tsp. brown sugar
1 slice of lemon
Sprinkle of cinnamon

Heat cider and brown sugar. Serve warm in a cup with lemon and cinnamon.

*By the time you realize how short life is
it's too late to apply the brakes.*

NOVEMBER 30

SESAME COOKIES

2 c. flour	1/2 c. shortening
1 c. sugar	2 eggs, beaten
1 tsp. baking powder	1 c. sesame seeds

Mix dry ingredients together, then add eggs and shortening. Mix ingredients well by kneading for 5 minutes. Roll into a long snake and cut into 1/8 inch circles. Pat each side of circle into sesame seeds. Bake at 300° for 20 minutes.

The motto for scouts is "Be Prepared". The motto for Girl Scout mothers should be "Be Prepared To Buy A Lot Of Cookies."

FEBRUARY 2

Sweet Potato Chips

2 sweet potatoes, peeled and sliced in 1/8" slices
1/4 c. butter, melted

Dip slices of potato into butter and place on cookie sheet. Bake at 425°
for 20 minutes. Let cool 5 minutes.

*It makes you wonder about the value of maturity
when you realize that children have sense enough
not to play football in the winter.*

NOVEMBER 29

HEART OF CREAM

8 oz. cream cheese,
softened
1/4 c. cream

1/3 c. powdered sugar
1 tsp. vanilla
Fresh fruit

Mix cheese, cream, sugar and vanilla together. Wet a piece of cheese cloth and spread it over heart shaped aluminum pan. Pour the cheese into the mold and cover with remaining cloth. Chill until firm. Unmold and serve with fresh fruit.

*Instead of loving your enemies, treat your friends
a little better.*

FEBRUARY 3

Walnut and Blue Cheese Pasta

9 oz. spinach pasta
2 T. butter
1 c. blue cheese, crumbled
1 c. walnuts, toasted and chopped

Cook pasta and drain. Toss with butter and sprinkle with blue cheese and walnuts.

*When people start treating you with respect,
you have to wonder if they know something about
your health that you don't.*

NOVEMBER 28

HEARTY BREAKFAST

1 slice bread
1 egg
1 tsp. butter
Heart shaped cookie cutter

Cut a heart shape out of a piece of bread. Heat butter in a pan and add the cut out bread piece. Crack an egg into the heart cut out. Cook until egg is set, then flip. Cook until browned.

One secret of longevity is to go to sleep in the same day you get up.

FEBRUARY 4

Chocolate Mix

1 c. chocolate chips, melted
6 c. popped popcorn
1 c. rice crispies
1/2 c. peanuts

Combine popcorn, cereal, and peanuts in a large bowl. Pour melted chocolate over popcorn and toss to coat. Spread on wax paper and cool.

*It's probably just as well you can't hang onto money
long enough to develop a real attachment.*

NOVEMBER 27

CANDY FLOWER

10 oz. candy melts
1/3 c. light corn syrup

Melt candy and add syrup. Mix well and pour out onto wax paper. Let harden for 4 hours. Shape dough into 10 marble-sized balls. Place on wax paper. Place another piece of wax paper on top and flatten each ball in a petal shape. Form the first petal as a rolled bud. Then shape petals around to form a flower.

One nice thing about a dull party is that you can get to bed at a decent hour.

FEBRUARY 5

MINI BAKED POTATOES

20 small red potatoes
1 c. sour cream
1/2 c. bacon bites

Wash potatoes and bake for 30 minutes at 350.° Cut in half and scoop out center with a spoon or melon baller. Mix with sour cream and bacon bits and fill the centers with mixture.

A grateful mind is a great mind.

NOVEMBER 26

PINEAPPLE SHAKE

1 small can crushed pineapple, drained
1 c. pineapple sherbet
1/2 c. pineapple juice

Combine pineapple, sherbet, and juice in a blender. Blend until well mixed. Serve immediately.

Whenever you are sincerely pleased, you are nourished.

FEBRUARY 6

TASTY TURKEY SANDWICH

2 slices of bread
1 slice of lettuce
1 slice hickory
    smoked turkey

1 tsp. chopped honey
    roast peanuts
1 T. plain yogurt
1 T. chutney

Combine peanuts, yogurt, and chutney. Place turkey and lettuce on the bread and top with yogurt mixture. Top with bread.

Thanksgiving is a day when the turkey gets stuffed in the morning and the family in the evening.

NOVEMBER 25

CRISPY TORTELLINI

8 oz. fresh tortellini
1/3 c. grated parmesan cheese
Salad oil
Salt

Place oil in pan to the depth of 1/2 inch. Heat oil to 350° . Place a small amount of tortellini in the oil and cook until crisp, turning occasionally. Place on paper towel to drain. Continue until all pasta is cooked. Sprinkle with parmesan cheese and salt to taste.

Too many cooks spoil the figure.

FEBRUARY 7

HOT BUTTERED LEMONADE

1/2 c. sugar
1/2 c. fresh frozen
   lemon juice

1 tsp. grated lemon peel
3½ c. water
1½ T. butter

Combine sugar, lemon juice, peel, and water in a saucepan and cook until hot. Pour into cups and dot with butter.

When future historians look at our TV listings for Thanksgiving day, they could easily come to the conclusion that what we're really thankful for is football.

NOVEMBER 24

ENGLISH MUFFIN PIZZA

1 English muffin, split
1/4 c. mozzarella cheese, grated
2 T. pizza sauce
4 slices pepperoni, chopped

Spread each side of the muffin with pizza sauce. Place pepperoni on top and cover with grated cheese. Heat in 350° oven for 10 minutes.

*Never miss an opportunity to make others happy –
even if you have to leave them alone to do it.*

FEBRUARY 8

CRANBERRY-RASPBERRY SAUCE

1 package fresh cranberries
1 package frozen raspberries in syrup
2/3 c. sugar

Combine all ingredients in a saucepan. Bring mixture to a boil, stirring.
Simmer for 10 minutes, cool, and serve.

*There is always one thing to be thankful for on Thanksgiving.
Be glad you're not a turkey!*

NOVEMBER 23

Tropical Chocolate Fondue

1/2 c. cream of coconut
1/2 c. chocolate chips
Tropical fruit

Combine the coconut cream and chocolate chips in a glass bowl and microwave for 3 minutes on 30% power. Stir until smooth. Serve warm with fresh pineapple and bananas for dipping.

To get ahead, don't wait for opportunity to knock before opening the door.

FEBRUARY 9

PUMPKIN CUSTARD

1/2 c. sugar
1 tsp. cinnamon
2 eggs
1 can pumpkin
1 tsp. vanilla

Combine sugar, cinnamon, eggs, milk, pumpkin and vanilla in the top of a double boiler. Stir over simmering water until custard thickens. Serve warm or cold over ice cream or cake.

Giving thanks is a course from which we never graduate.

NOVEMBER 22

PUFF PASTRY HEARTS

1 sheet frozen puff pastry, thawed
Heart shaped cookie cutter – floured

Unfold pastry and place on lightly floured board. Cut out hearts with cookie cutter. Place hearts on cookie sheet and bake in 450° oven for 10 minutes. Remove from oven and let cool. Cut in half and fill with sweet or savory filling.

We are told to love our enemies as well as our neighbors, probably because they are often the same people.

FEBRUARY 10

GRILLED POUND CAKE WITH MAPLE CREAM

2 slices of pound cake, about
1/2 inch thick
1/2 T. butter

1/3 c. whipped cream, or
topping
1 T. maple syrup

Melt butter in a sauté pan until bubbling, add slices of cake and sauté until brown turning once. Fold maple syrup into the whipped topping. Serve the grilled cake on a plate topped with maple cream.

What this country needs is a scale that takes off five pounds for good intentions.

NOVEMBER 21

MARBLED TEA EGGS

6 eggs
1 T. salt
2 T. soy sauce

1 whole star anise
1 tea bag

Hard cook eggs and gently tap shell to crack, but not remove. Mix salt, soy, anise and tea in 2 cups of water and bring to boil. Take off heat and add eggs in shell. Let sit in brine in refrigerator for 4 hours. Remove and shell.

*Some days we have to take three or four baths
to make the phone ring.*

FEBRUARY 11

ALMOND STUFFED DATES

20 pitted dates
20 blanched whole almonds
10 bacon strips

Stuff the dates with the almonds. Cut bacon strips into two pieces. Wrap each strip around each almond stuffed date. Place on paper towel lined plate and microwave for 2 minutes.

In our health conscious society, families count more calories than blessings.

NOVEMBER 20

WHITE GINGER TRUFFLE

10 oz. white chocolate, finely chopped
1/3 c. whipping cream
2 T. crystallized ginger, chopped
Powdered sugar

Combine chocolate and cream and heat to melt. Add ginger to mixture.
Cool in refrigerator until firm, about 4 hours. Scoop mixture into balls
and roll in powdered sugar.

*There is no substitute for good manners, except,
perhaps, fast reflexes.*

FEBRUARY 12

COOL PUMPKIN PIE

1 quart vanilla ice cream
1/2 c. pumpkin, canned
1/2 c. brown sugar
1 tsp. pumpkin pie spice
Prepared graham cracker pie crust

Combine ice cream, pumpkin, brown sugar and spice in a bowl. Pour into graham cracker crust. Place in freezer until firm.

A buffet dinner is one where the guests outnumber the chairs.

NOVEMBER 19

SLIM BAKED ALASKA

2 slices angel food, 1 inch thick cut in rounds
2 scoops frozen yogurt, flavor of your choice
2 egg whites
4 T. powdered sugar

Whip egg whites until soft peaks form and add sugar one T. at a time. Place a scoop of yogurt on each round of angel food. Frost with egg whites to cover. Place under broiler on low rack for 5 minutes. Serve immediately.

To be trusted is a greater compliment than to be loved.

FEBRUARY 13

BAKED PEARS WITH MACAROONS

4 ripe pears, peeled, cored and sliced
1/4 c. apricot preserves
4 macaroons, toasted and crumbled
3 T. butter

Place pears in a 9 inch round baking dish and spoon apricot jam on top. Sprinkle crumbled macaroons on top and dot with butter. Bake in a 375° oven for 20-30 minutes.

Don't complain about the cost of preparing a Thanksgiving meal – the pilgrims could have feasted on filet mignon.

NOVEMBER 18

LACE HEART

1 c. chocolate chips
1 T. shortening
Foil heart shape baking pan

Melt chocolate. Stir in shortening until smooth. Press aluminum foil into heart pan. Pour chocolate into a zip lock bag and cut off corner. Drizzle chocolate over bottom of pan in swirling motion. Refrigerate until set. Gently remove foil from pan and peel off.

All that is worth holding dear in this world begins in the heart, not in the head.

FEBRUARY 14

HOT PEPPER PECANS

2 T. butter, melted
1 c. pecans
2 tsp. soy sauce
1/4 tsp. pepper sauce

Toss pecans in melted butter and bake in a pan at 325° for 20 minutes. Combine soy and pepper sauce and toss into nuts. Drain on paper towel to remove excess moisture.

*If we are what we eat, then nuts must be
a bigger part of our diet than we think.*

NOVEMBER 17

LIGHT SPINACH DIP

1 package frozen
    chopped spinach,
    thawed and drained
1 c. plain low fat yogurt
1/2 c. onion, chopped

1/2 c. water chestnuts,
    chopped
1 tsp. dill weed
1 tsp. salt

Mix all ingredients and refrigerate. Serve with fresh vegetables or crackers.

No woman lives long enough to try all the recipes she clips out of the paper.

FEBRUARY 15

CHOCOLATE DIPPED APRICOTS

3 oz. chocolate, chopped and melted
16 Turkish apricots

Dip the apricots in the melted chocolate and place on a wax paper covered plate. Place in refrigerator until chocolate sets.

*Pride is the hardest thing to swallow even though
it's tasteless, colorless and sizeless.*

NOVEMBER 16

CHEESECAKE BROWNIES

1 box of brownie mix
12 oz. cream cheese, softened
1/2 c. sugar
2 eggs
2 T. lemon juice

Make brownies according to instructions. Pour in pan and bake for 10 minutes at 350.° Beat cheese and sugar together, then add eggs and lemon juice. Carefully spread over partially cooked brownies. Bake additional 20 minutes. Cool and cut into bars.

FEBRUARY 16

BROWNIE RAISIN SURPRISE

1 package brownie mix, prepared according to instructions
1 c. chocolate covered raisins

Add the raisins to the prepared brownie mix and combine. Put into pan and bake according to package instructions.

It is better to sleep on something before doing it than to do it wrong and stay awake worrying.

NOVEMBER 15

Cafe Au Lait

1/2 c. coffee, strong and hot
1/2 c. whole milk, hot
1 tsp. sugar

Combine and serve in a cup.

Don't laugh at others' coffee – you too may be old
and weak someday.

FEBRUARY 17

FRENCH TOAST SANDWICH

2 oz. mozzarella cheese, sliced
2 slices French bread
1 egg, beaten
1/2 T. butter

Make a sandwich with the cheese and bread. Dip in beaten egg and sauté in a pan with melted butter until golden.

Health food is something you nag your loved ones to death to eat.

NOVEMBER 14

VANILLA YOGURT CHEESE

8 oz. vanilla low-fat yogurt
Cheese cloth
Srainer

Line the strainer with wet cheese cloth. Pour in the yogurt and place over a bowl. Let liquid drain off in the refrigerator for 4 hours or until spreading thickness. Serve with crackers.

The best way to keep good deeds in memory is to keep them refreshed with new ones.

FEBRUARY 18

CORDIAL CUPS

4 oz. semisweet
    chocolate, chopped
1 T. shortening

Small foil cups
Whipped cream
Cordial

Melt chocolate and add shortening. Stir until smooth. Coat small foil cups with the melted chocolate using a spoon. Let harden in refrigerator and coat again. Peel off foil and fill with whipped cream or your favorite cordial. Float in hot coffee.

Optimist: someone who hasn't got around to reading the morning paper yet.

NOVEMBER 13

FRESH PINEAPPLE UPSIDE DOWN CAKE

1/2 fresh pineapple, cut
   into 1 inch pieces
1 tsp. ginger

1 c. brown sugar
1 stick butter
1 package yellow cake mix

Combine brown sugar, butter and ginger. Heat until bubbling. Place pineapple in the bottom of a greased 9 inch cake pan. Pour brown sugar mixture over the top. Prepare cake mix according to instructions, then pour over pineapple and sugar. Bake at 375° for about 30 minutes. Let cool about 10 minutes. Loosen cake from sides of pan and tip upside down on a platter.

FEBRUARY 19

RUSSIAN TEA

4 tea bags
3 c. boiling water
1 c. orange juice

1/4 c. honey
3 cloves
2 cinnamon sticks

Steep tea bags in boiling water for 5 minutes and then discard bags. Heat remaining ingredients in another pan and add to tea straining out the spices. Serve while hot.

Why is it that chipped dishes never break?

NOVEMBER 12

SOUTH OF THE BORDER EGGS

2 flour tortillas
10 oz. can Ro-Tel® (tomatoes and chili)

3 oz. monterey jack cheese, grated
2 eggs

Wrap tortillas in a paper towel and microwave for 20 seconds to soften. Press into custard cups and bake at 350° for 5 minutes. Sprinkle 1/2 cheese on the bottom of each tortilla. Cook Ro-Tel until reduced. Break eggs into pan and cook until set. Scoop eggs and tomatoes into tortilla shell and top them with remaining cheese. Bake for 2 minutes until cheese is melted.

It's all right to be an optimist, but no smart cook breaks an egg directly into the pan.

FEBRUARY 20

MICROWAVE PEANUT BRITTLE

1 c. sugar	1 tsp. butter
1/2 c. white corn syrup	1 tsp. vanilla
1 c. peanuts	1 tsp. baking soda

In a 4 cup measure, stir sugar and corn syrup together. Microwave on high for 4 minutes. Add peanuts. Stir and cook on high for 3½ minutes. Add vanilla and butter. Cook on high for 1½ minutes. Add baking soda. Stir and pour on lightly buttered jelly-roll pan. Cool and break into pieces.

Friends come in many different flavors.

NOVEMBER 11

GUACAMOLE

4 ripe avocados
3 T. salsa
1 T. lime juice
1 tomato, seeded and chopped
salt and pepper to taste

Mash avocados and add all ingredients.

The secret of success lies not in doing your own work, but in recognizing the right person to do it.

FEBRUARY 21

ARTICHOKE SPREAD

14 oz. can artichoke hearts, drained and chopped
1/2 c. mayonnaise
1/4 c. parmesan cheese, grated

Combine all ingredients in a bowl and chill. Serve with crackers.

*Some people have no trouble making ends meet –
their foot is always in their mouth.*

NOVEMBER 10

CARAMEL SAUCE

1 ½ c. brown sugar
1/2 c. butter
3 T. light karo syrup
1/2 c. cream

Heat brown sugar, butter and karo syrup in a pan. Bring to a boil, stirring constantly. Stir in cream and return to boil. Cool and serve over ice cream or fruit.

Counting time is not so important as making time count.

FEBRUARY 22

FOOTBALL BROWNIES

1 package brownie mix
1 tube white frosting
1 package chocolate frosting
Empty tuna can

Bake brownies according to instructions and cool. Press tuna can into an oval shape and use as brownie cookie cutter. Frost the footballs with chocolate frosting. Use white frosting tube to make football lacing.

Anyone who believes the way to a man's heart is through his stomach probably flunked geography.

NOVEMBER 9

ALMOND CREME

1 quart milk
2 packages of unflavored gelatin
1/2 c. water
1/2 c. sugar
1 T. almond extract

Soften gelatin in 1/2 c. water. Scald milk and add sugar, gelatin, and almond extract. Pour into pan and refrigerate until firm.

The quickest way to make a tossed salad is to feed vegetables to an 18-month-old child.

FEBRUARY 23

STROMBOLI

1 loaf of frozen white
    bread dough, thawed
12 fresh spinach leaves

1 c. mozzarella, grated
12 slices pastrami, or
    Virginia ham

Roll out bread dough until it forms a 12 by 9 rectangle. Place spinach, meat, and cheese on dough leaving an inch border. Roll up jelly roll fashion and seal seams. Place seam down on a cookie sheet. Bake at 350° for 30 minutes.

*Television enables you to be entertained in your home
by people you wouldn't have in your home.*

NOVEMBER 8

EASY CORN SALSA

1/2 c. canned corn, drained
1/2 c. salsa, your favorite

Combine and serve with tortilla chips.

*Some people bring more bills into their house
than a Congressman.*

FEBRUARY 24

ROQUEFORT "GRAPES"

8 oz. cream cheese
1/4 c. Roquefort cheese
Poppy seeds

Combine cream cheese and Roquefort. Roll into grape size balls and roll in poppy seeds. Cluster as a bunch of grapes and serve with crackers.

Anybody can win – unless there happens to be a second entry.

NOVEMBER 7

Piña Colada

2 T. coconut cream
3/4 c. pineapple juice
Slice of lemon
Crushed ice

Blend ingredients together and serve over crushed ice.

Who says nothing is impossible?
Some people have been doing it for years.

FEBRUARY 25

WALNUT BREAD

1 pkg. refrigerated uncooked pizza dough
3 T. bacon bits
1/2 c. chopped walnuts
1 T. olive oil

Unroll dough and brush with olive oil. Sprinkle with bacon and walnut and press into dough. Bake at 425° for 15 minutes.

Bread that has to be sliced with a saw is far too healthy.

NOVEMBER 6

STUFFED APPLE DELIGHT

3 apples, peeled and cored
3 T. honey
1/4 c. dates, chopped
1/4 c. walnuts, chopped

Combine dates and walnuts. Fill cavity of apples with mixture and pour honey over them. Bake in 325° oven for 35 minutes.

Doing little things well is a step toward doing big things better.

FEBRUARY 26

MOCA JAVA

1 c. hot chocolate
1 c. coffee
Whipped cream

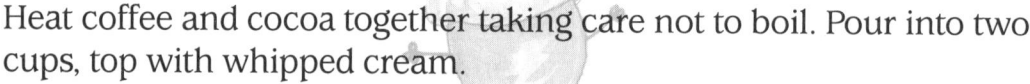

Heat coffee and cocoa together taking care not to boil. Pour into two cups, top with whipped cream.

Fact: the average coffee tree yields 1½ pounds of coffee in a year. Some people drink a tree in a day.

NOVEMBER 5

GARLIC LOVERS SPREAD

1 bulb garlic
1 T. oil
1/2 c. sour cream
1/2 c. cream cheese

Remove excess paper from bulb of garlic. Place whole bulb in foil and moisten with oil. Close foil tight and bake at 250° for 3 hours. Cut off top of bulb and squeeze out the garlic paste and mash. Blend with the sour cream and cream cheese.

If you have to eat your words, at least eat them while they are hot.

FEBRUARY 27

CURRIED DEVILED EGGS

6 eggs, hard cooked
3 T. mayonnaise
1/2 tsp. curry powder
1/4 tsp. salt

Cut eggs in half and gently scoop out yolks and mash. Add mayonnaise, curry powder, and salt and mix completely. Spoon mixture evenly into egg white shells.

No wonder a hen gets discouraged,
she can never find things where she laid them.

NOVEMBER 4

Phyllo Fruit Cup

3–4 inch squares of phyllo dough
vegetable oil spray

Spray each phyllo sheet with vegetable spray. Stack sheets on top of each other at an angle from the one below. Push squares into sprayed custard cup or muffin tin. Bake at 350° for 10 minutes. Fill with fruit.

*Be sure to hold your head high today,
but keep your nose at a friendly level.*

FEBRUARY 28

Salted Nut Roll

2 c. powdered sugar
7 oz. jar marshmallow creme
1 bag caramels, unwrapped and melted
3 c. salted nuts, chopped

Combine powdered sugar and marshmallow creme in a plastic bag and knead to mix. Divide dough into rolls of 1/4 c. each and freeze for 20 minutes. Dip into melted caramel and roll in chopped nuts. Wrap in plastic wrap and store in refrigerator.

Impossible challenge: to eat only one salted peanut.

NOVEMBER 3

NOW YOU SEE IT, NOW YOU DON'T

2 tsp. sugar
1 T. flour
1/2 tsp. cinnamon
2 T. butter, melted

8 marshmallows
1 roll refrigerated crescent
    roll dough

Combine sugar, flour and cinnamon. Dip marshmallow in butter and roll in flour mixture. Roll into 1 crescent triangle sealing seams carefully. Place in greased muffin tin. Bake at 375° for 15 minutes. Remove from tin and let cool. Then look for your marshmallow!

Miracle drug: Medicine children will take without screaming.

FEBRUARY 29

MINI CORN DOGS

16 precooked mini hot dogs
1 package refrigerated corn bread sticks

Cut corn bread sticks in half and wrap around a hot dog. Bake at 375°
for 10 minutes. Serve on a tooth pick.

*You can find your way across this country just by using
fast food restaurants the way navigators use stars.*

NOVEMBER 2

TANGY BACON

8 strips thick sliced bacon
1/2 c. brown sugar
1/4 c. mustard

Spread each piece of bacon with mustard. Sprinkle brown sugar over each piece. Place bacon on broiler rack and bake in upper third of the oven at 375° for 20 minutes.

Choose your party guests well, or you may be the most interesting person there.

MARCH 1

SLICED CARAMEL APPLES

1/2 c. Mrs. Richardson's® caramel sauce, or your favorite
1 apple, cored and sliced

Warm caramel in the microwave for 30 seconds. Pour over sliced apples.

An apple a day keeps the doctor away –
but an onion a day keeps everyone away.

NOVEMBER 1

GRAPEVINE CLUSTER

25 frozen dinner roll dough, thawed   1 egg, beaten

Arrange rolls on a greased cookie sheet in a grape bunch shape. Put several rolls on top of pyramid to give depth. Flatten 2 rolls in the shape of leaves and roll one roll in the shape of a stem. Place these pieces on the top of the grapevine. Paint the entire cluster with the egg wash. Bake at 325° for 20 to 25 minutes in the middle of the oven.

A well balanced person is one who finds both sides of the issue are laughable.

MARCH 2

CARAMEL COFFEE CAKE

1 loaf sweet roll dough, partially thawed
6 T. butter, melted
1/2 c. chopped nuts

3 oz. package regular butterscotch pudding mix
1/4 c. brown sugar

Generously butter bundt pan and sprinkle nuts. Cut partially thawed loaf into 24 pieces. Place pieces in pan. Sprinkle with pudding mix and brown sugar. Drizzle with butter. Cover and let rise in a warm place until double. Bake in a 350° oven for 25 minutes. After letting stand for 2 minutes, turn out onto a platter.

Nothing carries gossip faster than a sour grapevine.

OCTOBER 31

CHERRIES JUBILEE

1 can pitted black cherries
1 T. sugar
1/4 c. orange juice
2 tsp. corn starch

Heat cherries with juice in a saucepan with 1 T. sugar. Mix the cornstarch with the orange juice and add it to the warm cherries. Continue to cook until thickened. Serve warm over ice cream.

*Friendship is the only cement that will ever hold
the world together.*

MARCH 3

JOAN'S SWEET BAKED PUMPKIN

Small sugar pumpkin, cut off
top and seeded
2 c. apples, peeled and
chopped

1 c. raisins, dark & light
1 c. chopped walnuts
1 c. brown sugar
1 tsp. pumpkin pie spice

Place all ingredients in the cleaned pumpkin and place in shallow baking dish. Bake at 325° for 1 hour. Stir and bake another hour. Serve hot from the pumpkin over ice cream.

*Some people eat only from the three basic food groups –
canned, frozen and take-out.*

OCTOBER 30

Peanut Butter Cup Cookies

1 roll refrigerated peanut butter cookie dough
48 miniature peanut butter cups

Cut cookie dough into 1/4 inch slices. Press these slices into a greased miniature muffin tin. Then press a peanut butter cup into each cookie. Bake at 350° for 10 minutes.

Children are a great comfort in your old age – and sometimes they help you get there faster too.

MARCH 4

EDIBLE "SNAKES"

1 loaf frozen sweet
   roll dough
6 T. brown sugar

6 T. peanuts
6 T. chocolate chips
Vanilla frosting

Cut the thawed dough into 6 long strips. Flatten each strip out and sprinkle with 1 T. of each ingredient. Carefully roll and seal "snakes." Place carefully on a greased pan in a "snaky" position. Bake 20 minutes in a 350° oven. Frost with white frosting and sprinkle with colored sugar.

Why can't bad weather forecasts be wrong as often as the good ones.

OCTOBER 29

MUFFIN TOPS

Your favorite muffin mix with streusel topping

Make your favorite mix as directed, decreasing the liquid measure by 1/4 cup. Spoon 2-3 tablespoons of the mix on a greased cookie sheet and top with streusel. Bake 15 min. at 400°.

Many enjoy cooking – especially when it's done in a restaurant.

MARCH 5

CREEPY BAKED APPLE

1 apple
2 T. raspberry jelly
1 gummy worm

Core apple without going all the way to the bottom. Fill with jelly and bake for 25 minutes. Refill with jelly if it has all absorbed and place gummy worm in the opening.

Dietitians say if you eat slowly, you will eat less.
Anyone raised in a large family will tell you the same thing.

OCTOBER 28

WHOLE LEMON PIE

3 eggs
1 lemon, quartered
    and seeded
1½ c. sugar

3 tsp. lemon juice
1/3 c. butter, melted
1 unbaked pie shell

Combine eggs, lemon, (skin and all), sugar, juice, and butter in a blender. Process until smooth. Pour into unbaked shell and bake at 350° for 30 minutes.

The proof of the pie is in the amount of crust that is eaten.

MARCH 6

Jack-O-Lantern

Roll of refrigerated sugar
cookie dough

Candy corn
Life savers

Place a 1/2 inch thick round of dough on aluminum foil. Pat into 4 inch circle. Place candy on dough to form a face, making sure the candy is surrounded by dough. Bake for ten minutes in a 350° oven. Let cool completely before peeling off foil.

If you don't want your kids to listen to what you're saying, pretend you're talking to them.

OCTOBER 27

BLUEBERRY WHIP

2/3 c. milk
1/2 c. individually frozen blueberries
2 T. honey

Whip all ingredients in the blender at high speed. Serve immediately.

Why do people who shoot off their mouths never seem to run out of ammunition.

MARCH 7

HOT SPICED PUNCH

4 T. whole cloves
4 small oranges
1 gallon apple cider
3 cinnamon sticks

Press cloves into oranges and bake at 350° for 30 minutes. Heat apple cider in a large stock pot with oranges and cinnamon sticks.

Eat what you like and let your food settle the battle on the inside.

OCTOBER 26

EASTER BREAD BASKET

1 ½ loaves frozen bread dough, thawed
1 egg, beaten

Spray the bottom of a 9 inch round cake pan with vegetable spray. Take 1/2 of a loaf and press into the bottom of the pan. Take another loaf and cut it into three pieces. Roll and stretch each piece into a long snake. Braid these three "snakes" as you would strands of hair. Place this braid on top of the bread in the pan around the rim. Brush the entire bread basket with beaten egg. Bake at 325° for 25 minutes.

MARCH 8

LUXURY BREAD PUDDING

4 large stale croissants   2 eggs
2 c. milk   1/2 c. sugar
1/2 c. raisins

Tear croissants into bite-sized chunks. Combine croissant with milk and raisins until milk is absorbed. Combine eggs, vanilla, and sugar; pour custard into croissant mixture. Pour into buttered 9 inch glass baking dish. Bake in a 350° oven for one hour. Let cool and serve with whipped cream.

Balanced diet: what you eat at buffet suppers.

OCTOBER 25

Miniature Hot Dogs

1 package hickory smoked mini sausages
1 package breadstick dough

Brown the sausages in a sauce pan until done. Cut uncooked bread dough into pieces the size of the sausages. Cook the small breadsticks as directed on the package. Cut the mini bun in half and place sausage in the center.

Today families don't ask "What's cooking?" – instead they ask "What's thawing?"

MARCH 9

BREAD STICK BONES

1 roll of refrigerated breadstick bread dough

Lay each piece of dough out and tie a knot in each end. Place on cookie sheet and bake according to instructions.

Everyone believes in the golden rule: Give unto others the advice you can't use yourself.

OCTOBER 24

PINEAPPLE SALSA

1 small can crushed pineapple, drained
1/4 c. cream of coconut
2 T. lime juice
2 T. lime zest

Combine all ingredients together and heat in a microwave for 1 minute. Serve with ham or as a relish.

Difficult – That which can be done immediately.
Impossible – That which takes a little longer.

MARCH 10

CAROL'S HOT DOG OCTOPUS

Hot Dogs

Beginning one inch down from the end, make a cut through the length of the hot dog. Divide each strip in half and then in half again – all still attached to the top. Place in a pan of boiling water and watch the octopus grow!

Mealtime: when many youngsters sit down to continue eating.

OCTOBER 23

CHICKY BUNS

| 1 loaf sweet roll dough, thawed | Whole cloves Whole almonds |

Cut the dough lengthwise and roll into ropes that are 10 inches long and 1 inch wide. Tie the rope into a loose knot, leaving bottom end out and flatten for tail feather. Fold over top of knot to form a ball and press into knot to form a head. Make three slits with a knife tip in the head. Press in two cloves for eyes and an almond for the beak. Bake at 350° for 20 minutes.

Most of us take more than our daily requirement of vitamin "I".

MARCH 11

CURRIED PUMPKIN SEEDS

Pumpkin seeds from one pumpkin
2 T. vegetable oil
2 tsp. curry powder
1 tsp. salt

Toss pumpkin seeds with oil. Mix curry powder and salt together and sprinkle over seeds, toss to coat. Bake in 350° oven until the seeds are crisp.

*On those dreary rainy days, do you wonder
why anyone saves up for them?*

OCTOBER 22

DOUBLE ORANGE FLOAT

1/2 c. orange sherbet
1 c. orange juice

Scoop sherbet into a tall glass and fill with orange juice.

*It may take two to tangle –
but it also takes two to make up.*

MARCH 12

EASY RASPBERRY SAUCE

1 package frozen raspberries in syrup
2 T. of sugar

Thaw raspberries and add sugar. Pour thawed berries with juice into a sieve. Use a wooden spoon to push the berry pulp through the sieve leaving the seeds behind.

*Remember the teakettle – when it's up to its neck
in hot water it sings.*

OCTOBER 21

SLIM APRICOT SOUFFLÉ

1 egg white
1 T. sugar
1 T. apricot jam

Beat egg white until it foams, then add sugar and continue to beat until it forms stiff peaks. Fold in the apricot jam. Spoon into a large custard dish that has been sprayed with vegetable oil. Bake in a 400° oven for 10 minutes. Sprinkle with powdered sugar and serve hot.

*Success is the ability to get along with some people
and ahead of others.*

MARCH 13

ALMOND APPLE SAUCE

2 lb. cooking apple, peeled, cored and chopped
1/2 c. sugar
2 T. cream
1/4 tsp. almond extract

Cook apples in a covered pan over low heat for about 20 minutes. Add sugar and cook for 5 minutes more. Stir in cream and almond extract.

A success is a failure with a fresh coat of paint.

OCTOBER 20

MEATBALL APPETIZERS

1 lb. ground beef
1 c. breadcrumbs
1 egg
1/2 c. onions, chopped
Salt and pepper to taste

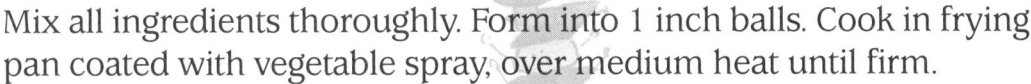

Mix all ingredients thoroughly. Form into 1 inch balls. Cook in frying pan coated with vegetable spray, over medium heat until firm.

It is more important to know where you are going
than to get there quickly.

MARCH 14

Maple Leaf Toast

8 slices of pumpernickel
2 T. melted butter
1/3 c. grated parmesan cheese

Make a cut out of a leaf on a bread sized piece of paper. Brush bread with melted butter. Place leaf cutout over the bread and sprinkle cheese over cutout, then lift off cutout carefully. Bake in 450° oven for 5 minutes.

You know food prices are going up when pumpernickel is now called pumperdime.

OCTOBER 19

SWEET AND SOUR SAUCE FOR MEATBALLS

1/2 c. maple syrup
1 T. balsamic or cider vinegar
1 tsp. Dijon mustard

Mix all ingredients together and pour over warm meatballs. Heat thoroughly and serve.

*Perhaps the reward of those who try is not the goal
but the exercise*

MARCH 15

Tex Mex Cornbread

1 package cornbread mix
3 T. canned chilies
1 small can whole kernel corn
3 T. cheddar cheese, shredded

Mix the cornbread according to package instructions. Add the chilies, corn, and cheese and bake according to package instructions.

Nobody can give you wiser advice than yourself.

OCTOBER 18

Easter Baskets

12 oz. vanilla candy coating

Melt the candy coating. Pour melted coating into a plastic bag. Cover the outside of 6 custard dishes with foil. Cut a small hole in the filled bag and drizzle the coating in a circular motion over the foil covered custard dishes. Chill until set and remove foil.

Lord, grant that I may desire more than I can accomplish.
~ Michelangelo

MARCH 16

ORANGE WHIP ANGEL CAKE

1 slice angel food cake
1 T. orange marmalade
1/4 c. whipped cream, or whipped topping

Fold the marmalade into the whipped topping and serve on top of angel food slice.

People who blow a fuse are usually in the dark.

OCTOBER 17

St. Patty's Pie

                1 bag miniature   2 c. whipping cream,
                    marshmallows   whipped
                1/4 c. milk   1 chocolate cookie pie
                1/4 c. green mint syrup   crust

Melt marshmallows with milk over low heat. Add mint syrup, mix and cool. When the mixture is room temperature, fold in whipped cream. Pour mixture into cookie crust and freeze. Thaw 15 minutes before serving.

*Blessed are the hard of hearing,
for they miss much small talk.*

MARCH 17

MEGAN'S SPECIAL HOT CHOCOLATE

1 c. hot chocolate, your favorite
1 Rondo® or any chocolate covered ice cream morsel

Drop the ice cream into the hot chocolate and stir as it melts.

A child is someone who knows all the questions at eight and all the answers at eighteen.

OCTOBER 16

EASTER EGG TRUFFLES

1/3 c. cream
10 oz. white chocolate, chopped
1 tsp. almond extract

Heat all ingredients until melted. Chill for 4 hours until hardened.
Spoon out and shape as eggs. Roll in pastel colored sugars.

*If absence makes the heart grow fonder –
then a lot of people certainly love church.*

MARCH 18

Roasted Almond Balls

1 c. heavy cream
12 oz. semisweet
   chocolate

2 T. strong coffee
2 c. almonds, roasted
   chopped

Heat cream and add chopped chocolate. Stir until chocolate is melted. Add coffee and stir in one cup toasted chopped almonds. Chill for 4 hours until firm. Form into tablespoon sized balls and roll in remaining almonds.

In today's world a mint is not what you eat after dinner, but what you need to pay the restaurant bill.

OCTOBER 15

BIRD'S NESTS

1 c. chocolate chips, melted
3 oz. chow mein noodles
1 c. jelly beans

Pour melted chocolate chips over chow mein noodles and stir to coat. Drop the mixture by the tablespoon onto a baking sheet covered with wax paper. Make an indentation in each to create a nest and drop in several jelly beans. Chill to set.

No one should live by the early bird policy without first finding out whether they classify as a bird or a worm.

MARCH 19

GINGERSNAP ICE CREAM SANDWICHES

16 gingersnaps
1 pint ice cream

Place 2 T. of ice cream on the flat side of 8 gingersnaps. Place remaining gingersnaps on top and press in place. Eat at once or wrap in plastic wrap and freeze for later.

Food prices are changing our way of life. Parents may soon say, "eat your dessert or you won't get any meat."

OCTOBER 14

CHOCOLATE MALT SYRUP

1 c. sugar
1/2 c. cocoa
1/4 c. water
1/2 c. malt powder

Combine all ingredients until smooth. Cook over low heat until the mixture comes to a boil. Turn heat to its lowest setting and continue to cook for three minutes. Cool and refrigerate for up to three weeks.

When the going gets tough – the tough eat chocolate.

MARCH 20

BUCK EYES

2½ c. powdered sugar
1 c. crunchy peanut
    butter
1/2 c. melted butter

1 tsp. vanilla
12 oz. chocolate
    chips, melted

Thoroughly mix powdered sugar, crunchy peanut butter, butter, and vanilla. Chill to set up. Roll into balls. Insert a tooth pick in the chilled ball and dip half way into melted chocolate. Set on wax paper to harden.

The best thing to hold onto in today's world is each other.

OCTOBER 13

Potato and Bacon Pizza

1 pkg. refrigerated pizza
dough
1 T. olive oil
5 red potatoes, thinly
sliced

5 slices bacon, cooked
crisp
3 T. parmesan cheese

Roll out dough and spread with potatoes. Brush potatoes with oil. Sprinkle on bacon and parmesan cheese. Bake in lower part of 400° oven for 25 minutes.

It used to be that two could live as cheaply as one; now one can live as expensively as two.

MARCH 21

MAPLE FRAPPE

1 c. French vanilla ice cream
1/4 c. milk
1 T. maple syrup

Put all ingredients into blender and blend until smooth.

Nothing stimulates one's appetite like an empty wallet.

OCTOBER 12

CHEWY CHOCOLATE PIE

1 stick margarine, melted
2 oz. chocolate chips, melted
1 c. sugar
2 eggs, beaten
1/2 c. flour
1 T. vanilla

Mix all ingredients together. Pour the mixture into an 8 inch greased pie plate. Bake in a 350° oven for 30 minutes.

Tact: Getting your point across without stabbing someone in the back.

MARCH 22

HAM ROLL UPS

1 T. Dijon mustard
1 T. apricot jam
1/4 c. cream cheese
10 slices baked ham

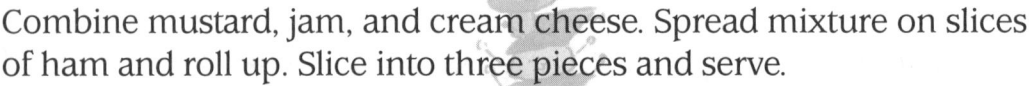

Combine mustard, jam, and cream cheese. Spread mixture on slices of ham and roll up. Slice into three pieces and serve.

Since we don't always know which side our bread is buttered, some people play safe by eating both sides.

OCTOBER 11

SEAFOOD CRESCENTS

1 roll refrigerated crescent roll dough
8 seafood sticks

Unroll the crescent dough and cut each triangle in half. Cut each seafood stick in half and place the sticks on each of the triangles. Roll up and bake according to instructions on the package.

A fish is an animal that seems to go on vacation about the same time most fishermen do.

MARCH 23

UPSIDE DOWN PEAR PIE

4 pears, peeled, cored
and halved
1 c. sugar

1 pkg. refrigerated
single pie crust
dough

In oven proof skillet heat sugar on medium setting, stirring occasionally, until it melts and becomes a caramel color. Add pears to pan cut side up. Heat pears through, then place the pie crust on top tucking edges inside pan. Bake in a 425° oven for about 25 minutes. Cool about 10 minutes and turn over onto platter.

*Success consists not in never failing,
but in rising every time we fall.*

OCTOBER 10

CRUMMY PEACHES

1 can peaches in heavy syrup, drained
1 c. crumbled butter cookies
Butter flavored vegetable spray

Place drained peaches in the bottom of a shallow pan. Top with the butter cookie crumbs. Spray with the butter flavored spray. Bake at 375° for 20 minutes.

There are two doors to opportunity – push and pull.

MARCH 24

GRILLED APPLE CHEESE SANDWICH

2 slices bread
3 slices apple, peeled
and cored

1 slice Swiss cheese
1 tsp. Dijon mustard
Butter

Melt butter in a pan and sauté apple slices for about a minute. Remove apple and place on bread with cheese. Cover and grill in pan with the apple flavored butter turning once until the cheese is melted and the bread is toasted.

Steering committee: Three people trying to park a car.

OCTOBER 9

Jam Tarts

1 package pie crust mix
Assorted jams

Make pie crust according to instructions on the package. Roll out to 1/8 inch thick. Using a small round cookie cutter, cut out circles in the dough. Press the rounds into mini muffin tins and top with a teaspoon of your favorite jam. Bake in a 375° oven for 10 minutes. Cool until jam is solid and remove from muffin tin.

Love is an itch around the heart that you can't scratch.

MARCH 25

APPLE SPRITZER

1/2 c. apple juice
1/2 c. lemon lime soda
Cinnamon stick

Fill a glass with ice cubes, add apple juice and soda. Stir with a cinnamon stick.

When you're in deep water, it's best to keep your mouth shut.

OCTOBER 8

PINEAPPLE DRESSING

1/4 c. butter, melted
1/2 c. sugar
1 small can crushed pineapple, drained
10 slices white bread, cubed

Combine all the ingredients and bake in a greased uncovered casserole at 350° for 1 hour. Great with poultry or ham.

With the price of fresh fruit these days, it's almost cheaper to fly to Hawaii than buy a pineapple.

MARCH 26

TROPICAL BAGEL

1 bagel, split
2 T. cream cheese
2 pineapple rings, drained
2 T. coconut

Toast bagel and spread halves with cream cheese. Place one pineapple ring on each half and sprinkle with coconut.

Some people can dish it out – but they can't cook it.

OCTOBER 7

HAYSTACKS

6 oz. white chocolate
1 c. shredded sweetened coconut

Melt chocolate. When melted, add the coconut and blend. Drop on wax paper by the teaspoon. Refrigerate until set.

It may be harder for a rich man to get into heaven, but it's easy for him to get on the church board of trustees.

MARCH 27

SAUTÉED PEARS

2 ripe pears, peeled, cored and sliced
2 T. butter
1/4 c. brown sugar

Melt butter in a sauté pan. Add pears and brown sugar. Cook over medium heat until pears are soft and sauce is caramel color.

The world would be a better place if we were surrounded by more open minds and fewer open mouths.

OCTOBER 6

FROSTED POUND CAKE

1 c. whipped topping
1 package instant pudding – your favorite flavor
1 c. milk
1 pound cake

Make pudding according to instructions. Fold in the whipped topping.
Cut the cake in half and then frost bottom. Place the other half on top
and frost the whole cake. Chill and serve.

*Money can't buy happiness –
but it sure makes shopping more fun.*

MARCH 28

Pizza Popcorn

1 bag microwave popcorn, butter flavored
1 T. Italian spice mix – or oregano
3 T. grated parmesan cheese

Microwave popcorn according to instructions. Pour popped popcorn into a bowl and toss with spices and cheese.

*Teenagers don't really have any hang-ups –
everything they own is usually on the floor.*

OCTOBER 5

PINEAPPLE SURPRISE JUICE

1 c. pineapple juice
1 c. tomato juice
1/4 tsp. salt
1/2 c. crushed ice

Blend all ingredients and serve immediately.

Looks can be so deceiving – people should be made up like food packages with all the ingredients clearly listed.

MARCH 29

Sunrise Fruit Drink

2 tsp. grenadine syrup
1/2 c. orange juice
1/2 c. pineapple juice

Place 1 tsp. grenadine syrup in the bottom of a wine glass. Fill with ice and add orange juice and pineapple juice. Add another T. of grenadine to the top.

An ounce of performance is worth an ounce of preachment.

OCTOBER 4

CREAMY JELLO®

1 package Jello, flavor of your choice
3/4 c. boiling water
3/4 c. evaporated milk

Make the Jello using the 3/4 c. boiling water and evaporated milk.

*Antiques are the things one generation buys,
the next generation gets rid of, and the following
generation buys again.*

MARCH 30

MINI MAC'S

12 vanilla wafers
6 chocolate-covered
   peppermint patties

1/4 c. vanilla frosting, dyed
   with red food coloring
Water
Sesame seeds

Place 6 of the vanilla wafers, flat side up, on a cookie sheet. Top each wafer with a peppermint patty. Place in 325° oven until chocolate begins to soften, about one minute. Place a dollop of frosting on top and top with another wafer. Brush top with water and sprinkle with sesame seeds.

A smile is a wrinkle that shouldn't be removed.

OCTOBER 3

Chocolate Marshmallow Bars

6 oz. chocolate chips
3/4 c. peanut butter
6 oz. butterscotch chips
1/2 bag miniature marshmallows

Melt chips and peanut butter on low heat, stirring constantly. Remove from heat and add marshmallow. Pour into a greased 9 inch square pan and refrigerate.

Rule of life: If you're in a hole, stop digging.

MARCH 31

Yogurt Sundae

8 oz. vanilla yogurt, fat and sugar free
1/4 c. granola
1/3 c. grapes, sliced

Layer yogurt, granola, and grapes (or fruit of choice).

*It's easy to stick to a diet these days –
just eat what you can afford.*

OCTOBER 2

Raspberry Fool

1 10 oz. package frozen raspberries, thawed
2 c. whipping cream
2 T. sugar

Drain thawed raspberries reserving the juice for another use. Whip the cream with the sugar. Fold in raspberries creating marble effect and serve.

There's no fool like an old fool who's managed to outlive the rest.

APRIL 1

STUFFED FIGS

12 large dried figs, cut in half
1 c. cream cheese
1/4 c. walnuts, toasted and chopped

Combine walnuts and cream cheese. Scoop about 1/2 T. of mixture into each half of fig.

*What people like best about their mother's cooking
is that is doesn't cost them anything.*

OCTOBER 1

Raspberry Soda

1/4 c. juice from frozen raspberries
8 oz. ginger ale

Combine 1/4 c. raspberry juice with an 8 oz. glass of ginger ale. Serve over ice.

Ginger ale: a drink that tastes the way your foot feels when it's asleep.

APRIL 2

CARAMEL GRAHAM CRACKER COOKIES

12 graham cracker
squares
1 stick of margarine

1/2 c. brown sugar
1/2 c. chopped pecans

Melt the margarine in a heavy saucepan, add sugar and bring to a boil, stirring constantly. Pour mixture over graham crackers lined in a jelly roll pan. Sprinkle with nuts. Bake in a 350° oven for 10 minutes. Cut and cool.

Life is like a bath; a wrong turn can leave you in hot water.

SEPTEMBER 30

"Hamburger" Cakes

1 package yellow cake mix	1 package brownie mix
1 can cherry frosting	Empty tuna cans

Prepare cake and brownie mix according to instructions. Grease tuna cans and pour in cake batter to 1/3 full. Bake as directed for muffins. Pour brownies into a 12 x 8 inch pan so they remain thin and bake 20 minutes. Cut in circles using tuna can as cutter. To assemble, cut cake in half and place brownie on the bottom. Spread cherry frosting on the brownie and place top on cake. Sprinkle with sesame seeds.

A contented person enjoys the scenery on a detour.

APRIL 3

MEXICAN HOT CHOCOLATE

1 c. hot chocolate of your choice
1/2 T. cinnamon
1 dash nutmeg
Dollop of whip cream

Add spices to the hot chocolate and top with whipped cream.

*To make a fortune today, you have to
come up with something that is low priced, habit forming
and tax-deductible.*

SEPTEMBER 29

"FRENCH FRIES"

1 roll sugar cookie dough
Aluminum foil

Cut a three inch log of cookie dough. Cut the log in half and each half into thirds forming six wedges. Fold aluminum foil into an accordion pleat, grease and place on cookie sheet. Place cookie wedges on foil and bake according to instructions.

Praise not only pretends that we are better than we are; it may help to make us better than we are.

APRIL 4

HOT CHEESE DIP FOR A CROWD

2 lb. box Velveeta® cheese
8 oz. prepared salsa

Add ingredients to a crock pot and heat through.

There is always free cheese in the mousetrap.

SEPTEMBER 28

New Idea Pizza

Baked pizza crust
10 spears frozen asparagus, thawed
1 c. monterey jack cheese, grated
1/4 c. pimento strips

Spread cheese on pizza crust and top with asparagus and pimento. Bake for 10 minutes in a 450° oven.

*Conscience doesn't keep you from doing anything;
it merely keeps you from enjoying it.*

APRIL 5

EASY APPLE DUMPLINGS

1 tube refrigerated biscuits
10 apple slices
2 T. butter
4 T. cinnamon sugar

Flatten each biscuit into a large circle. Dredge apple slices in cinnamon sugar. Place each slice on a flattened circle, fold and pinch. Paint with butter and sprinkle with remaining cinnamon sugar. Bake at 400° for 10 minutes.

Achieve and you will have no need for ancestors.

SEPTEMBER 27

SLIM AND TRIM TRIFLE

1 loaf angel food cake
1 qt. strawberries, sliced

2 c. low fat vanilla yogurt
2 c. light whipped topping

Cut the cake into 1 inch cubes. Place a layer of cake in a glass bowl, top with a layer of strawberries, then yogurt, then cool whip. Continue layering until ingredients are gone.

The best sellers in many book stores are cook books and diet books. One tells you how to prepare your food – the other tells you how not to eat your food.

APRIL 6

PEANUT BUTTER STICKS

1/2 c. peanut butter
1/4 c. dry milk
1 T. honey
Sesame seeds

Mix peanut butter, milk, and honey together. Form into sticks and roll in sesame seeds.

Many kids show signs of being a successful executive –
they already take two hours for lunch.

SEPTEMBER 26

Pecan Stuffed French Toast

4 oz. cream cheese	3 eggs, beaten
3 T. sugar	1 loaf French bread
3 T. pecans, chopped	

Blend cream cheese, nuts, and sugar. Cut bread into one inch slices. Then slice a pocket in the center of each. Spoon about 1 tablespoon of the cheese mixture into each pocket. Dip each slice into eggs and fry until golden, turning once. Serve with maple syrup.

It's easy the night before to get up early the next morning.

APRIL 7

PEAR GINGERBREAD

2 pears, peeled and chopped or canned, drained
1 gingerbread mix, prepare according to instructions

Place prepared batter in 9 inch pan according to instructions. Spread chopped pears evenly over top. Bake 35 minutes.

Every year it takes less time to fly across the ocean than it does to drive to work.

SEPTEMBER 25

HOMEMADE PEANUT BUTTER

2 c. unsalted roasted peanuts
1/4 tsp. salt

Place ingredients in a food processor bowl and process until spreadable. Pour into a container and chill until ready to serve.

One nice thing about children is that they don't keep telling you boring stories about the clever things their parents said.

APRIL 8

APRICOT CREAM CHEESE

1/4 c. dried apricots, chopped
3 T. orange juice
1 c. light cream cheese
3 T. honey

Soak apricots in orange juice for about 10 minutes. Combine cheese, honey, and apricot juice mixture. Serve with fruit or crackers.

It is often the last key which opens the door of opportunity.

SEPTEMBER 24

STUFFED RADISHES

12 radishes, halved
4 oz. cream cheese
1/2 c. black olives, pitted and minced
1 T. capers, minced

Hollow out each half of the radish with a small melon baller. Mix together cream cheese, olives, and capers. Spoon 1 teaspoon into each of the halves.

Life is like a buffet – some things may not be great,
but there's plenty of it.

APRIL 9

SPICED TEA

4 c. boiling water
4 tsp. loose tea
6 whole cloves
1/2 tsp. dried orange peel
1/8 tsp. ground cinnamon

Pour boiling water over tea, cloves, orange peel and cinnamon in a teapot. Cover and let steep 5 minutes. Strain before serving.

Autumn is when the leaves slowly turn from green to gold to work.

SEPTEMBER 23

CUPCAKE CONES

1 package chocolate cake mix   Vanilla frosting
Flat bottom ice cream cones   Sprinkles

Prepare cake mix according to instructions. Fill cone with mix to 2/3 full. Place cones on baking sheet and bake according to instructions for cupcakes. When cool, frost and sprinkle.

*The great thing about cake mixes is that
future generations will have no trouble making treats
just like mom used to make.*

APRIL 10

Breakfast To Go

2 frozen waffles, toasted
1 slice Canadian bacon, grilled
1 fried egg
1 slice cheese

Put bacon on one waffle and top with egg and cheese. Put second waffle on top.

When you feel dog tired at night maybe it's because you growled all day.

SEPTEMBER 22

PICKLE ROLLS

5 large dill pickles
5 slices ham
1/4 c. cream cheese

Spread softened cream cheese on each ham slice. Place pickle at the end and roll up. Chill until chilled. Slice into 1/2 inch rounds and serve.

Wouldn't it be simpler if we just spell it "orderves".

APRIL 11

SOUTH OF THE BORDER WON TONS

Won ton wrappers
Vegetable oil spray
Salsa

Arrange won tons on baking sheet. Spray with oil and bake at 350° for about 5 minutes or until crispy. Serve with salsa.

*Most TV dinners taste like they have been prepared
by the TV repairman.*

SEPTEMBER 21

OLIVE LOAF

1 loaf whole wheat bread dough, thawed
1/2 c. pimiento stuffed olives, drained

Roll out dough into a rectangle. Spread olives on the dough. Then roll up the dough, seal the seams and let rise for about 30 minutes. Bake in a 350° oven for 30 minutes.

Big food companies are working on a tearless onion, and they probably can do it – they've already given us tasteless bread.

APRIL 12

MAKE YOUR OWN CANDY BARS

1 c. chocolate chips
1/2 c. raisins
1/2 c. chopped salted peanuts

Melt chocolate and add the raisins and peanuts. Spoon mixture on wax paper in 4 bars. Chill until firm.

Using a microwave without directions is like trying to parallel park a tank.

SEPTEMBER 20

BANANAS FOSTER

4 bananas, sliced
1/4 c. butter
1/4 c. brown sugar
1 T. lemon juice

Melt butter and brown sugar in a pan. Add the bananas and lemon juice and cook until heated through. Serve warm over ice cream.

Some people have such big mouths they can eat
a whole banana – sideways.

APRIL 13

Coconut Macaroons

Parchment or wax paper
2 egg whites
1 c. powdered sugar
3 c. coconut

Whisk the egg whites until stiff. Whisk in the sugar, then fold in the coconut. Pile the mixture in 12 pyramid shapes on the parchment. Bake at 325° for 25 minutes, or until golden brown.

Before you can score you must first have a goal.

SEPTEMBER 19

LEMON COKE

1 cola drink
1 slice lemon

Fill glass with coke and ice. Squeeze lemon slice into it.

The rule before all others heed,
Have ready everything you need
before you start, be sure to read
the recipe – then work with speed.

APRIL 14

Apple Pizza

1 pkg. refrigerated
   single pie crust dough
5 baking apples, cored,
   peeled and sliced

1/2 c. brown sugar
1/2 c. nuts
1/2 c. cheddar cheese,
   grated

Roll out pie crust to fit 12 inch pizza pan and bake at 425° for 10 minutes. Place apples on crust and sprinkle with brown sugar and nuts. Bake for 20 minutes at 400°. Remove from oven and sprinkle on cheese. Cut in wedges and serve.

The problem with being the most popular student in school is that the other kids hate you for it.

SEPTEMBER 18

Bologna Egg Cup

1 slice bologna
1 egg
1/4 c. cheddar cheese

Heat bologna in a pan until it puffs in the center. Place the cooked bologna in a custard cup, crack an egg into it and sprinkle cheese on the top. Bake in a 375° oven for 15 minutes or until egg has set.

April is the month that tells us not only is Washington's face on our money – but Washington's hands are on it as well.

APRIL 15

Banana Delight

1 banana, peeled
1/2 c. mini chocolate chips
1 T. whipped topping
1 T. chopped nuts

Create trench down the center of the banana. Fill this trench with chocolate chips. Microwave for about 50 seconds until the chips are melted and the banana is hot. Serve with cool whip and chopped nuts.

The secret of success is a secret to most of us.

SEPTEMBER 17

CHUTNEY CREAM CHEESE

1 bottle of your favorite chutney
8 oz. cream cheese

Place cheese on platter and pour chutney over it. Serve with crackers.

American cooking is the art of taking food containers and putting them on plates.

APRIL 16

PIGLETS IN A BLANKET

24 small smoked sausage links
1 can refrigerated crescent rolls

Cut each crescent into three pieces. Wrap each piece around sausages. Place in 375° oven and bake for 15 minutes.

*If you have leftover meat and potatoes,
why not make dejà stew?*

SEPTEMBER 16

SMOKED SALMON PATÉ

4 oz. smoked salmon
8 oz. cream cheese
2 T. capers
1/4 c. red onion, diced

Chop salmon into small pieces. Combine ingredients and mix until blended. Serve with thin sliced dark rye.

Rule of life: Never do anything you can't talk about after dinner.

APRIL 17

VIVIAN'S JAM CUPCAKES

1 c. flour	2 eggs
1 c. sugar	Milk
1 tsp. baking powder	Jam
1/4 c. melted butter	

Mix dry ingredients together. Pour butter in 1 cup measure, add 2 eggs and fill to 1 cup with milk. Add to dry ingredients and blend. Pour into muffin tin and bake at 350° for 25 minutes. Cut cone shaped hole in the top, fill hole with favorite jam and replace cone.

Many of us will do everything to shorten our lives, then pay a doctor to tell us to stop.

SEPTEMBER 15

LEMON SHERBET IN LEMON BOWL

4 lemons
1 pint lemon sherbet

Slice off top third of the lemon and scoop out the pulp. Cut a small slice off the bottom to let it set upright. Fill the lemon with lemon sherbet and put on the lid. Serve immediately or freeze until later.

If you think time heals everything, try sitting it out in a doctor's office.

APRIL 18

ORANGE MILKSHAKE

1 c. milk
1 c. orange sherbet

Pour milk in blender; add sherbet. Whip until frothy.

*Success in life is making promises and keeping them.
Promises to yourself, and promises to others.*

SEPTEMBER 14

White Chocolate Fondue

6 oz. white chocolate, chopped
1/2 c. miniature marshmallows
1/4 c. whipping cream
2 T. butter

Combine all ingredients. Heat until melted. Serve with fresh fruit for dipping.

Americans don't spend millions for amusement. They spend it in search of amusement.

APRIL 19

Low Fat Cheese Puffs

15 mozzarella cheese cubes - 1/2 inch in size
1 egg, slightly beaten
1/2 c. Italian bread crumbs

Dip cheese cubes in egg, then roll in bread crumbs. Dip and roll again.
Bake at 425° for 5 minutes.

The world is divided into people who do things,
and people who get the credit.

SEPTEMBER 13

TOAST CUPS

12 slices white bread, crusts trimmed
4 T. butter, melted

Brush bread with melted butter and press into muffin cups. Bake in a 350° oven for 20 minutes or until golden.

Some day someone is going to make a fortune putting out a breakfast cereal that will drain the energy from kids!

APRIL 20

Cashew Truffles

10 oz. milk chocolate, chopped
1/3 c. cream
1 c. cashews, unsalted and chopped

Scald cream, remove from heat and add chocolate. Cover until melted. Stir until smooth and add nuts. Chill until firm and form into balls. Dip in melted chocolate or roll in chopped cashews.

The most expensive vehicle to operate by the mile, is the shopping cart.

SEPTEMBER 12

SOMETHING TO FILL TOAST CUPS

8 oz. mushrooms, chopped
1 T. butter
1/4 onion, minccd
1/4 c. sour cream

Melt butter in pan and add onions, cook until soft. Add mushrooms and cook until lightly brown. Take off heat and stir in sour cream. Serve in toast cups.

Those who stay on the level rise higher in the end.

APRIL 21

GRILLED PB AND J

2 pieces of bread
1 T. peanut butter
1 T. jelly
2 tsp. butter

Make a peanut butter and jelly sandwich as you usually would. Butter the outsides of the sandwich and grill in a pan. Serve warm.

Maybe parents would enjoy their children more
if they stopped to realize that this
is one film you can't rewind and play again.

SEPTEMBER 11

TURTLES

1/2 c. caramels
48 pecans
1/4 c. chocolate, melted

Melt caramels and pour 1 to 2 teaspoons over 4 pecans placed in a cross pattern on wax paper. Let the caramel cool and harden. Spoon 1 teaspoon of chocolate on each and cool until hardened.

It would help if scientists would figure out how our bodies turn a couple ounces of chocolate into five pounds of fat.

APRIL 22

PEARS AND BLUE CHEESE

2 pears, peeled, halved and cored (or canned)
2 T. blue cheese, crumbled
1/4 c. cream cheese

Combine blue cheese and cream cheese. Fill the cavity left by the pear core.

Wisdom is the reward you get for a lifetime of listening when you'd have preferred to talk.

SEPTEMBER 10

Seafood Roll

1 medium hard roll
2 seafood sticks
2 T. mayonnaise
2 tsp. capers

Cut bun in half and scoop out each soft bread center. Spray with vegetable spray and toast until lightly brown. Spread each half with mayonnaise. Cut seafood stick in 4 pieces and stack in each half. Sprinkle with capers and serve.

Give a man a fish and you feed him for a day. Teach a man to fish, and he's gone every weekend.

APRIL 23

ALMOND QUESADILLAS

1 flour tortilla
1/4 c. jack cheese, shredded
2 T. smokehouse almonds, chopped
Salsa

Place cheese on tortilla and top with almonds. Heat under broiler until cheese is melted. Cut into wedges and serve with salsa.

A life spent worthily should be measured by deeds, not years.

SEPTEMBER 9

DUSTY ROAD

2 scoops chocolate ice cream
2 T. chocolate malt powder

Sprinkle ice cream with the malt powder and serve.

The world is composed of givers and takers. The takers may eat better – but the givers sleep better.

APRIL 24

INSTANT DONUTS

1 package refrigerated biscuit dough
2 c. oil
1/2 c. sugar

Make a hole in the middle of each uncooked biscuit with a small cutter. Heat oil and test with a donut hole – if it bobs to the surface immediately, oil is ready. Fry biscuits until light brown turning once. Drain on paper towel and roll in sugar.

A pessimist is one who only sees the hole in the doughnut.

SEPTEMBER 8

BLUE CHEESE CORN BREAD

1 package corn bread mix
1/2 c. blue cheese, crumbled
2 green onions, chopped

Prepare the corn bread according to instructions. Add blue cheese and onions and mix to combine. Bake for 30 minutes in a 350° oven.

Some guests stay longer in an evening than others stay in a week.

APRIL 25

Peanut Butter Cupcakes

12 mini peanut butter cups, foil removed
1 package fudge brownie mix

Line muffin tin with muffin papers sprayed with vegetable oil spray.
Prepare brownie mix as label directs, and spoon into muffin papers.
Place a candy on top of each cupcake and bake according to package
instructions.

*There are only two things that matter in life – chocolate and,
oh dear, what was the other one?*

SEPTEMBER 7

PALMIERS

1 sheet frozen puff pastry dough, thawed
1/2 c. sugar

Spread the sugar on unfolded dough and roll lightly to press sugar into dough. Roll the two sides to the middle as a scroll. Cut into 1/2 inch slices and bake for 20 minutes in a 375° oven, turning once.

Don't be afraid to be different – you may be better that way.

APRIL 26

BOSTON COOLER

1 c. ginger ale
2 scoops vanilla ice cream

Scoop ice cream into a tall glass and carefully pour over the ginger ale.

*In this world , it is not what we take up, but what we give up
that makes us rich.*

SEPTEMBER 6

TEA AND FRUIT CUP

1 c. hot tea
1-2 T. sugar
1 c. assorted dried fruit

Combine all ingredients and let set over night in the refrigerator. Serve for breakfast.

Successful people are those who do what they have to do at the time they hate to do it most.

APRIL 27

PARMESAN TOASTS

2 large pita breads
Vegetable oil spray
3 T. grated parmesan cheese

Cut each pita in half making 2 rounds. Spray inside with oil and sprinkle with parmesan cheese. Place on cookie sheet under broiler for 2 minutes. Cut in wedges and serve.

The stomach is the commanding part of the body.

SEPTEMBER 5

CHOCOLATE SOUP

1 c. whipping cream
1 tsp. instant coffee
10 oz. semisweet chocolate

Bring cream and coffee to boil in a pan. Take off heat, add chocolate and stir until melted. Divide into small bowls and serve with pieces of fruit and cake for dipping.

When opportunity knocks, most people are out in the yard looking for four-leaf clovers.

APRIL 28

ZUCCHINI CAKE

1 c. grated zucchini
1 spiced cake mix
1/4 c. less water than called for

Add zucchini to cake mix and blend. Add reduced amount of water.
Bake according to instructions.

*You can always spot people with few friends. They're the
ones buying zucchini in the grocery store.*

SEPTEMBER 4

Surprise Toast Topper

1 slice whole wheat bread, toasted
1 slice bacon, cooked crisp
1/4 c. prepared guacamole

Top toast with guacamole and chopped bacon.

Friendship consists in forgetting what one gives and remembering what one receives.

APRIL 29

LACY CHEESE WAFER

Cheddar cheese in 1/2 inch cubes

Line a cookie sheet with parchment paper or microwave paper. Place cheese cubes two inches apart on cookie sheet and place in oven at 350° for 5-7 minutes. Let cool for two minutes and then remove wafers with a spatula to a rack.

Canapés are a sandwich cut into 24 pieces.

SEPTEMBER 3

CRAB DIP

1/2 stick of butter
6 oz. Velveeta® cheese
1 can crabmeat

Melt cheese and butter, mix until smooth and creamy. Stir in crab meat.
Serve with chips.

Good cooking is like good painting – it can be tasted,
but not explained.

APRIL 30

APPLE OMELETTE

1 cooking apple, peeled,
    cored, and chopped
1 T. butter

2 T. brown sugar
2 eggs, separated
3 T. sugar

Sauté apples with brown sugar and butter in oven proof skillet. Whip egg whites until stiff. Mix sugar and egg yolks, then add to whites. Pour mixture over apples and bake at 450° for 10 minutes.

If you don't work with enthusiasm, you'll be fired with enthusiasm.

SEPTEMBER 2

SLIM CHERRY SODA

1 can diet cherry soda
2 scoops frozen cherry yogurt

Place one scoop of frozen yogurt in a tall glass. Pour soda into the glass, then add the other scoop. Serve with a spoon and straw.

*Exercise is what some do to loosen up
but often end up falling apart.*

MAY 1

CARAMEL NUT DIP

1 c. softened cream cheese
1/4 c. caramel topping
1/3 c. chopped honey roasted nuts

Mix ingredients together. Serve with fruit for dipping.

Why is it the person who doesn't want to go to the party is the one who is the last to leave?

SEPTEMBER 1

Phyllo Cookie Rolls

3 sheets phyllo dough
6 T. butter, melted
6 T. sugar

6 T. sliced almonds,
finely chopped

Spread out the phyllo dough and paint with 2 T. butter. Sprinkle with 2 T. sugar and almonds and cut sheet in quarters. Tightly roll up each square and cut into two inch lengths. Repeat with the remaining sheets. Brush with butter and bake in a 350° oven for 10 minutes.

The best preparation for tomorrow is the right use of today.

MAY 2

PEANUT BUTTER CAKE

1 single layer white cake mix
1/4 c. crunchy peanut butter
Prepared chocolate frosting
1/2 c. peanuts, chopped

Prepare cake according to instructions. Then add peanut butter and pour into prepared pan. Bake and cool. Frost and sprinkle with chopped peanuts.

The best inheritance parents can give their children is a few minutes of their day.

AUGUST 31

Flower Pots

3 small new clay flower pots
6 frozen dinner roll dough, thawed
Aluminum foil
Artificial flowers

Shape the aluminum foil over the bottom of the pot, then place it in the pot and spray with vegetable spray. Place two dinner rolls in each pot and let rise. Bake according to instructions. Place artificial flower in each pot.

The happiest people are those too busy to notice.

MAY 3

BLINIS

8 oz. package cream
    cheese, softened
1/4 c. sugar
1 egg yolk

1 loaf thin sliced white
    bread, crusts removed
1/2 c. butter, melted
Cinnamon sugar

Combine cream cheese, sugar, and egg yolk into a smooth mixture. Flatten slices of bread with a rolling pin and spread with cream cheese mixture. Roll jelly roll fashion and dip in melted butter, then roll in cinnamon sugar. Freeze until solid. Bake frozen in a 400° oven for 10 minutes or until golden. Serve hot.

What a big gap there is between advice and help.

AUGUST 30

MELON BITES

1 honeydew melon
1 cantaloupe
3 oz. thinly sliced ham

Cut each melon in half and scoop out seeds. Use a melon baller to scoop out pulp from each melon. Cut ham into 1/2 inch strips and wrap each strip around the melon ball. Fasten with a toothpick and serve.

If you want a place in the sun you have to expect a few blisters.

MAY 4

ZUCCHINI PIZZA

4 medium zucchini, sliced 1/2 inch thick
1 c. pizza sauce
1/3 c. chopped black olives
1 c. shredded cheese.

Arrange zucchini slices on a greased baking sheet. Top each slice with sauce, then olives and cheese. Place under broiler for 5 minutes or until top is brown, but zucchini is still crisp. Serve warm.

The bigger the summer vacation, the harder the Fall.

AUGUST 29

Rainbow Cookies

1 package refrigerated sugar cookie dough
Red, blue, green and yellow food coloring

Divide dough into four equal parts. Place each portion in a plastic bag and add a different color in each. Knead until blended. Form dough into rectangle and place one on top of the other. Refrigerate until firm and slice into 1/8 inch pieces. Bake in a 350° oven for 10 minutes.

If you can't remember what worried you last week you haven't any troubles.

MAY 5

GRILLED LEMON CHICKEN

4 boneless chicken breasts, cubed
Frozen lemonade concentrate, thawed
4 skewers
1 T. olive oil

Brush chicken with olive oil and skewer. Place on hot grill and brush
frequently with concentrated lemonade. Cook about 10 minutes or
until cooked through.

*The law of success: more bone in the back
and less in the head.*

AUGUST 28

CINNAMON HEARTS

1 can soft breadstick dough
1/2 c. sugar
1 tsp. cinnamon

Roll breadstick dough in the cinnamon sugar mixture. Shape into a heart on a cookie sheet. Bake according to instructions.

When love and skill work together, expect a masterpiece.

MAY 6

HONEYDEW BISQUE

1 honeydew, peeled, seeded and diced
2 c. lime sherbet
2 T. lime juice

Combine all ingredients in a blender, reserving 1/2 c. honeydew, and process until smooth. Serve immediately in bowls. Top with chopped melon.

*If only we'd stop trying to be happy,
we'd all have a pretty good time.*

AUGUST 27

COOKIE ICE CREAM ROLLS

1 pint rocky road ice cream, in a cylinder container
1/2 c. chocolate chip cookie crumbs
1/2 c. chocolate sauce

Cut the ice cream container to remove ice cream in a whole roll. Place crumbs on wax paper and roll ice cream over them to coat. Freeze until hard. Slice and serve with chocolate sauce.

Work is the main course of life – pleasure the dessert.

MAY 7

BLUE CHEESE BURGER

1 lb. ground beef
4 T. crumbled blue cheese
4 buns

Divide ground beef into 8 thin patties. Place 1 tablespoon of blue cheese on top of 4 of the patties and top with the remaining patties, sealing the edges. Place burgers in pan or on top of grill and cook 10 minutes or until done, turning once. Serve on buns.

Why is it those who can wait 3 hours for a fish to bite can't wait 5 minutes for dinner?

AUGUST 26

CHEESY FRENCH TOAST

1 loaf French bread
4 oz. cheddar cheese, in slices
2 eggs, beaten

Cut French bread into 1 inch slices. Cut a pocket into each slice and place a piece of cheese into it. Dip each slice into egg and fry until golden on both sides and serve.

Don't agonize over giving up the good for the great.

MAY 8

POPPY SEED SKILLET CAKE

1 pound cake mix, prepared according to directions
2 T. poppy seeds
1 T. grated orange rind

Mix all ingredients together and pour into well greased skillet or loaf pan. Bake according to instructions on the package. Cool and serve.

Some people pay a compliment as if they expect a receipt.

AUGUST 25

Apricot Rose

5 dried apricot halves

Place apricot halves between sheets of wax paper. Roll until flattened with a rolling pin. Remove an apricot and roll into tight bud. Then place other halves around bud and bend back edges to look petal like. Secure with a toothpick.

When travel doesn't broaden the mind,
it lengthens the conversation.

MAY 9

ICED CAFE LATTÉ

2 c. cold coffee
2 T. cream
2 T. sugar
1/4 tsp. cinnamon

Combine all ingredients and pour over ice into two glasses.

Good coffee keeps more people awake than a bad conscience.

AUGUST 24

White Chocolate Pecan Truffles

10 oz. white chocolate, chopped
1/3 c. heavy cream
2 c. pecans, toasted and chopped

Heat cream and chocolate until melted. Add 1 cup chopped pecans and stir until blended. Chill until set about 4 hours. Form into balls and roll into chopped pecans to coat. Serve or refrigerate.

You will never be hurt by anything you don't say.

MAY 10

HERBED BUTTER

1 stick butter, softened
2 T. fresh herb of choice, minced
1 T. red onion, finely minced

Combine all ingredients and chill until firm. Use mixture to top grilled meats, fish, or vegetables.

The only sure thing about luck is that it will change.

AUGUST 23

VANILLA DIP FOR BERRIES

4 oz. cream cheese, softened
1/4 c. sugar
1 c. vanilla yogurt

Blend all ingredients until smooth and serve with assorted fruit for
dipping.

Trying times are times for trying.

MAY 11

RED PEPPER JELLY

2 large red bell peppers, seeded and chopped

1¼ c. vinegar
3 c. sugar
1 pouch liquid pectin

Place peppers in a blender and process until pureed. Blend with the vinegar and sugar in a large pan. Bring to a rolling boil, stirring constantly. Pour in pectin and bring to boil again and boil for one minute more. Pour hot jelly into sterilized jars and seal.

The probability of the bread falling jelly side down is directly proportional to the cost of the carpet.

AUGUST 22

HUMMUS – MIDDLE EASTERN DIP

1/4 c. sesame seeds toasted
1 c. garbanzo beans
3 T. lemon juice
2 cloves garlic
3 T. olive oil

Drain beans saving 6 T. of liquid. Add all ingredients in blender or processor and whirl until smooth. Serve with pita bread.

*Lettuce is like conversation; it must be fresh and crisp,
so sparkling that you scarcely notice the bitter in it.*

MAY 12

WATERMELON PEAKS

1/4 watermelon, cut in wedges
1 c. white chocolate, melted

Pour two tablespoons of white chocolate on each of the peaks. Place in refrigerator until hardened and serve.

A good storyteller is one who has a good memory and hopes other people haven't.

AUGUST 21

PITA CRISPS

8 small pitas
1/4 c. olive oil

Split the pita in half and brush with oil. Cut the pita into wedges and bake in a 375° oven until crisp, about 5 minutes.

*Appetizers: the little bits you eat until you
lose your appetite.*

MAY 13

"ANGEL FOOD"

1 pound cake, cut in one inch squares
1 can sweetened condensed milk
1 package shredded coconut
Skewers

Dip the cake in the milk and roll in coconut. Place on skewer and place on grill away from direct heat. Turn until golden on all sides.

When company stays too long just treat them like family, and they'll soon leave.

AUGUST 20

ORANGE ICE TEA

4 c. ice tea
4 c. orange juice

Combine ice tea and orange juice. Chill and serve over ice. Add sweetening to taste.

People usually get somewhere when they develop a brake for the tongue and an accelerator for the brain.

MAY 14

ZUCCHINI FRITTERS

3 c. zucchini, grated　　　1/4 c. parmesan cheese,
2 eggs, beaten　　　　　　　grated
1 T. flour

Combine eggs, flour and parmesan cheese. Pour mixture over the zucchini and stir to combine. Drop the zucchini batter by the tablespoonful into a hot pan sprayed with vegetable oil spray. Cook until golden on one side and turn to cook until golden on the other side. Serve warm.

A baby-sitter is a teenager who gets paid two dollars an hour to eat ten dollars worth of food.

AUGUST 19

Root Beer Cake

1 package single layer white cake mix
1 package vanilla frosting
1 can root beer
1 T. root beer extract

Make cake mix according to instructions, substituting root beer for the liquid and bake. Add root beer extract to the frosting and blend. Frost cooled cake with root beer frosting.

*Some people's idea of an eight-course dinner is
a seven layer cake and coffee.*

MAY 15

PESTO DEVILED EGGS

8 hard boiled eggs
2 T. pesto
1 T. mayonnaise

Halve the eggs and remove the yolks. Mash the yolks in a bowl and blend in the pesto and mayo. Fill the egg white shells with the mixture and serve.

A hen is an egg's way of making another egg.

AUGUST 18

Raspberry Mousse

1 package frozen red raspberries, thawed	1 package unflavored gelatin
1 c. cream	2 T. water

Sprinkle gelatin on water and let soften. Press berries through a sieve to remove seeds. Heat puree in a pan and add softened gelatin, bring to a boil. Remove from heat and let cool. Whip cream and fold in cooled berry mixture. Refrigerate until set.

*Good manners is making company feel at home –
even when you wish they were.*

MAY 16

ALMOND CHOCOLATE APRICOTS

25 Turkish dried apricots
1/4 c. almond paste
1 c. chocolate chips, melted

Open each apricot up with a slit in the seam. Press 1/2 T. almond paste into opening and press the apricot closed. Dip the apricot into chocolate and place on a wax paper covered cookie sheet. Refrigerate until the chocolate is hard.

If you can get people laughing you can tell them almost anything.

AUGUST 17

RHUBARB BETTY

4 c. rhubarb, cubed	3/4 c. flour
1 c. sugar	3/4 c. brown sugar
3/4 c. oatmeal	1 stick butter, melted

Toss rhubarb with sugar. Combine oatmeal, flour, brown sugar and butter. Press 1/2 the mixture in a 9 inch pan, add the rhubarb mixture. Top with remaining oatmeal mixture. Bake in a 350° oven for 40 minutes.

When the world laughs at you, laugh back;
it's just as funny as you are.

MAY 17

HOT DOG ON A STICK

8 hot dogs
1 package of refrigerated breadstick dough
8 skewers

Place hot dog on a skewer. Wrap the dough around the hot dog. Cook on the side of the grill away from the direct heat turning frequently until breadstick and hot dog are cooked.

*Raising children is like making bread;
you have to take your time or you end up with a tough crust
and an underdone interior.*

AUGUST 16

ASPARAGUS BURRITOS

8 asparagus spears
4 flour tortillas
4 slices Swiss cheese

Cook asparagus in a pan of boiling water for 3 minutes, then rinse in cooled water. Place cheese on tortilla and two spears of asparagus. Roll and heat in 350° oven until cheese is melted.

Do you ever feel like some weeks have five Mondays?

MAY 18

Nutty For Peaches

1/2 c. pecans, toasted and chopped fine
2 T. brown sugar
2 peaches, dipped in boiling water and peeled

Halve the peaches and discard the pit. Roll peach halves in a mixture of pecans and brown sugar. Place on a plate cut side down and serve.

*Some people are so busy that the only time they take
a vacation is when they sit down to eat.*

AUGUST 15

Chocolate Chip Meringues

4 egg whites
3/4 c. sugar
6 oz. mini chocolate chips

Beat egg whites on medium speed until foamy. Continue beating and gradually add sugar. Fold in the chips. Drop the mixture by the spoonful on parchment paper covered cookie sheet. Bake for 1 hour in a 250° oven.

If you wish to gain success, do not stare up the steps –
step up the stairs.

MAY 19

How Now Slim Cow

1 can diet root beer, cold
2 scoops chocolate frozen yogurt

Place one scoop of yogurt in a tall glass. Pour the root beer over the scoop, then add the remaining scoop. Serve with a spoon and straw.

If you are overweight you may have a medical problem –
you may be retaining ice cream.

AUGUST 14

Sweet Broiled Grapefruit

1/2 grapefruit, sectioned
1 T. brown sugar

Spoon the brown sugar over the fruit and place under broiler until heated through.

The world could use a grapefruit that can yell, "Fore" !

MAY 20

GRILLED CORN WITH BACON

1 ear of corn in husk
1 strip of bacon

Pull back the husk, but keep it attached to the ear. Remove the silk and soak the corn in water for 30 minutes. Wrap bacon around the ear and replace the husk. Place on grill and cover. Cook for 30 minutes, turning once. Remove husks and eat.

We have lost everything if we have lost our enthusiasm.

AUGUST 13

Chocolate Peanut Swirl

8 oz. white chocolate chips
6 oz. chunky peanut butter
4 oz. chocolate chips, melted

Add peanut butter to the white chips and heat until melted. Stir until smooth. Pour mixture onto wax paper. Pour melted chocolate chips over it and swirl it through with a knife. Chill until firm. Cut into small squares.

*Good deeds and hot bubble baths are the best cure
for depression.*

MAY 21

COOKIE SHORTCAKE

2 chocolate wafer cookies
Your favorite berries
Whipped topping

Place whipped topping on the cookie and top with fruit and the other cookie.

*Vacation time: that period when the flowers
in your garden are in full bloom and only the neighbors
are home to enjoy them.*

AUGUST 12

PEPPERMINT SHAKE

1 c. vanilla ice cream
1/2 c. milk
3 peppermint hard candies, crushed

Add all ingredients to a blender and process until smooth.

The trouble with fast talkers is that they may say something they haven't thought of yet.

MAY 22

DIPPED CHIPS

1 bag ripple chips
1 c. white chocolate or coating, melted

Dip each chip into the chocolate to cover about 1/2 of chip. Set on wax paper covered cookie sheet. Chill for a minute until set.

*The only way to entertain some people is to listen
to everything they say.*

AUGUST 11

HEATH CREAM CAKE

1 c. cream, whipped
3/4 c. Heath candy pieces
Pound cake

Fold candy pieces into whipped cream and serve on slices of pound cake.

O weary mothers mixing dough,
Don't you wish that food would grow?
Your lips would smile I know to see
A cookie bush or a pancake tree.

– unknown

MAY 23

STRAWBERRY CLUB SANDWICH

3 slices pound cake
3 T. strawberry cream cheese
1/4 c. strawberries, sliced

Spread two slices of the pound cake with the cream cheese and place the strawberries on top of the cream cheese. Stack the pound cake slices and top with plain slice. Cut diagonally and serve.

Success comes to those who hustle while they wait.

AUGUST 10

RHUBARB UPSIDE DOWN CAKE

3 T. butter, melted
1/2 c. sugar
2 c. rhubarb, finely diced

1 package single layer
white cake mix

Combine butter, sugar and rhubarb and spread in a 9 inch cake pan. Prepare cake mix according to instructions and pour over fruit. Bake in a 375° oven for 30 minutes. Loosen edges and invert pan on plate. Lift off pan and serve.

*No one can have everything – there isn't
that much closet space!*

MAY 24

ORANGE SWIZZLER

1 orange
1 candy stick

Roll orange to release juice. Poke a small hole in the skin with a knife. Push the candy stick into the hole. Use candy stick as straw to draw up the juice.

*Summer camps; those places children go
for their parents' vacation.*

AUGUST 9

PULL APART LOAF

3 c. Swiss cheese, grated
1 Vienna loaf
1/2 c. butter, melted

Cut bread the long way with a serrated knife 3/4 of the way down the loaf and 1 inch apart. Then cut across the loaf making cuts 1 inch apart. Stuff the cheese around each square. Pour melted butter over the loaf, wrap in foil and bake in a 350° oven for 30 minutes. Unwrap and pull apart to serve.

Your ship won't come in until you row out to meet it.

MAY 25

CROSTINI

1 c. basil, chopped
1 tomato, seeded and
    chopped
1 garlic, minced

1 small can minced black
    olives, drained
1/2 c. grated parmesan cheese
1 loaf French bread, sliced

Combine first five ingredients. Spread the mixture on the slices of French bread and place on baking sheet. Place the baking sheet under broiler and toast for 3 minutes.

*Parsley is a restaurant's idea of decoration
and a means of diverting your attention from the small
portion on your plate.*

AUGUST 8

Summer Truffle

10 oz. white chocolate, melted
1/3 c. cream
2 T. orange zest
Powdered sugar

Combine chocolate, cream, and orange zest. Chill until firm. Scoop into balls and roll in powdered sugar.

Believe only half of what you hear, but make sure it's the right half.

MAY 26

RASPBERRY SMOOTHIE

1 c. raspberries
1 c. buttermilk
1 banana, peeled and sliced
2 T. honey

Combine all ingredients in a blender and mix until smooth. Serve in tall glass.

Just because someone says, "Dutch Treat," doesn't mean they want to take you to Amsterdam.

AUGUST 7

SPAGHETTI OMELETTE

2 c. cooked spaghetti,
rinsed and cool
1 egg

1/4 c. mozzarella, grated
1 T. olive oil
Spaghetti sauce

Mix spaghetti with egg. Heat frying pan with oil and press 1/2 the spaghetti into it. Add the grated cheese and top with remaining spaghetti. Cook until golden on the bottom and flip. Continue to cook until golden. Cut with pizza cutter and serve with warm sauce.

*The trouble with eating Italian food is that
five or six days later you're hungry again.*

MAY 27

SPICY YOGURT CUCUMBERS

Cucumbers, peeled and sliced
1 c. plain yogurt
2 T. fresh cilantro, chopped
1 tsp. cumin seeds

Mix yogurt, cilantro, and cumin together. Refrigerate for at least 20 minutes before serving. Spoon over cucumbers and serve.

*The grass may be greener on the other side of the fence –
but so is the water bill.*

AUGUST 6

DIRT CUPS

1 package chocolate mousse mix, prepared
1 package chocolate water cookies, crushed
Gummy worms

Place a layer of cookie crumbs in the bottom of 8 small paper cups.
Top with a layer of mousse. Repeat layer. Press gummy worms into
mixture and top with cookie crumbs.

Frustrated parent to child at dinner:
"Eat it dear, just pretend it's mud."

MAY 28

Seafood Pizza

1 baked pizza crust
8 oz. cream cheese
6 seafood sticks, chopped
2 tomatoes, seeded and chopped
1/4 c. black olives

Spread cream cheese on cooled pizza crust. Sprinkle remaining ingredients over the top.

*It's all right to have a train of thought
if you also have a terminal.*

AUGUST 5

TOMATO JUICE SMOOTHIE

1/2 c. tomato juice
1/2 c. plain yogurt

Blend yogurt and tomato juice and serve.

Life is too short to stuff a cherry tomato.

MAY 29

EASY SHORTCAKE

1 tube refrigerated biscuit dough
2 T. sugar
2 T. butter, melted

Separate the biscuit dough. Brush each top with butter and then sprinkle sugar. Place on a greased cookie sheet and bake according to instructions. Split the cooked biscuits and top with fruit.

Wouldn't it be great if you could bang a tube against the counter and a five course meal popped out?

AUGUST 4

COFFEE CREME

2 c. hot coffee
1/4 c. sugar
1/2 c. whipped topping

1 package unflavored
gelatin, softened
over 2 t. water

Add gelatin and sugar to hot coffee and bring to a boil. Divide 1 cup of mixture into 4 wine glasses. Refrigerate until firm. Cool remaining mixture until slightly thickened, then beat with electric mixture until frothy. Pour frothy mixture over gelatin in wine glasses. Top with whipped topping.

*The caffeine doesn't keep you awake anymore –
now it's the price of coffee.*

MAY 30

LIME SHAKE

1 pint vanilla ice cream
1/3 c. limeade concentrate

Place the ice cream and limeade concentrate in a blender. Process until smooth. Serve in a tall glass.

Summer is when people come back from their vacation to rest up on their job.

AUGUST 3

FRUIT PIZZA

1 roll refrigerated sugar
cookie dough
8 oz. package cream
cheese, softened

1/4 c. sugar
4 c. assorted fruit

Slice cookie dough into 1/8 inch slices and press slices onto greased pizza pan to form a crust. Bake according to instructions. Blend cream cheese and sugar. When crust is cool spread with mixture of cream cheese and sugar. Place fruit on top in decorative circles. Slice like a pizza.

What do you do if an apple a day costs more than the doctor?

MAY 31

Taco Burgers

1 lb. ground beef
1 package taco mix
Prepared salsa
Sour cream
Buns

Combine ground beef and taco mix. Form into patties and place on grill to cook through. Top hamburgers with salsa and sour cream.

Anyone can separate hamburger when it's thawed.
But it takes the right stuff to attack it frozen at 5:30 p.m.

AUGUST 2

RHUBARB CUSTARD PIE

4 c. rhubarb, chopped
2 c. sugar
1/4 c. flour

3 T. milk
1 pie crust, unbaked
3 eggs

Combine flour, milk and eggs until smooth. Toss rhubarb with sugar and add to custard. Pour into unbaked pie shell and bake in a 400° oven for one hour.

The best thing to put in a homemade pie is your teeth.

JUNE 1

CANDY CRUNCH ICE CREAM

1 pint vanilla ice cream, slightly softened
Your favorite candy bar, chopped

Mix ice cream and chopped candy bar. Return to freezer until firm.

Just when children get old enough for parents to tolerate them, they can't tolerate their parents.

AUGUST 1

Double Butter Sundae

2 scoops butter pecan ice cream
3 T. butterscotch sauce

Place ice cream in a sundae glass and top with sauce.

*Ant – a small insect, though always at work,
still finds time to go to picnics.*

JUNE 2

Plum Preserves

1 c. red plums, pitted and chopped
1/2 c. sugar

Combine plums and sugar. Either microwave on high for 10 minutes, stirring after five minutes or heat on stove in heavy pan until mixture boils and thickens. Keep refrigerated.

*Opinions that are well rooted should grow
and change like a healthy tree.*

JULY 31

LEMON ICE CREAM

1 c. sugar   2 c. half and half
7 T. fresh lemon Juice

Mix sugar and juice together. Slowly add the half and half. Pour into an 8 inch pan and place in freezer for 1½ hours. Stir after the first 45 minutes and the second 45 minutes. Keep in freezer until ready to serve.

Summer is the time when you try to keep the house as cold as it was in the winter when you complained about it.

JUNE 3

STRAWBERRY SOUP

2 c. strawberries, hulled and sliced
8 oz. strawberry yogurt
1/2 c. sugar
1 T. lemon

Place all ingredients in a blender and puree until smooth. **For a colorful treat pour peach and strawberry soup into each side of a bowl simultaneously. Garnish with whipped cream and strawberry slice.

Sunshine is the best of all disinfectants.

JULY 30

SWEET HOT!!! MUSTARD

1 can dry mustard
1/2 c. white wine vinegar
1/2 c. sugar
1 egg

Mix all ingredients together and heat over low heat until slightly thickened. Cool and store in the refrigerator until ready to use.

*The only thing worse than being talked about,
is not being talked about.*

JUNE 4

PEACH SOUP

2 peaches, pitted and sliced
8 oz. peach yogurt
1/4 c. sugar
1 T. lemon

Place all ingredients in a blender and puree until smooth. Refrigerate until ready to serve.

Etiquette is the noise you don't make when you eat soup.

JULY 29

REUBEN ROLLS

1 package refrigerated
  crescnt roll dough
Mustard
16 cocktail franks

1/2 c. sauerkraut, rinsed
  and drained
Caraway seeds

Separate dough into triangles and cut each in half. Spread with mustard and top with sauerkraut and one cocktail frank. Roll to enclose and dip top in caraway seed. Bake according to instructions.

Do not complain that roses have thorns,
just be glad thorns have roses.

JUNE 5

HAMBURGER ON A STICK

1/4 lb. ground beef
1 skewer
1 hot dog bun

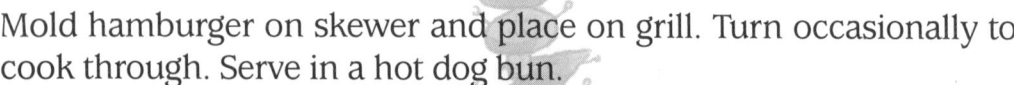

Mold hamburger on skewer and place on grill. Turn occasionally to cook through. Serve in a hot dog bun.

*Leftovers is food that is here tomorrow –
and the next day too.*

JULY 28

PEPPERMINT BROWNIES

1 package brownie mix
1 c. Junior Mints®

Mix brownies according to directions. Add the Junior Mints to the mix and pour into a 9 inch pan. Bake according to directions.

Tact is the business of handling porcupines without disturbing the quills.

JUNE 6

BETSY'S PEACH HONEY

1 c. peaches, peeled, pitted and mashed
1 c. sugar

Combine sugar and peaches and bring to boil stirring constantly. Then reduce heat and simmer until thickened. Seal in hot sterilized jars.

The early bird catches the worm – and he's welcome to it!

JULY 27

STRAWBERRY FLOWERS

Whole strawberries
Aerosol whipping cream

Cut the stem end off the strawberries to create a flat surface. Make three cross cuts from the tip 3/4 of the way down the strawberry. Open slightly and place whip cream rosette in the open cross.

The best way to distinguish between weeds and flowers is to cut them all down – those that come back are the weeds.

JUNE 7

Grape "Bon Bons"

Grapes

Remove grapes from stem. Wash and dry, then place on plate in the freezer. When frozen solid place in plastic bag and store. Eat the grapes like guilt free bon bons.

Dieting is something we do religiously. We eat what we want and pray we don't gain weight.

JULY 26

GRANDMA'S AMBER SAUCE

1 c. brown sugar
1/2 c. dark corn syrup
1/2 stick butter
1/3 c. cream

Bring brown sugar, syrup and butter to a boil for 2 minutes. Add cream. Cool and serve over cake or ice cream.

*A garden is something you can't live off of
without almost living in.*

JUNE 8

POTATO CHIP CHICKEN KABOBS

4 chicken breasts, boneless and skinless
1/2 c. sour cream
2 c. potato chips, crushed
4 skewers

Cut each breast into 5 pieces. Dip each piece in sour cream, roll in crushed chips and place on skewers. Wrap each stick in aluminum foil and place on grill for about 25 minutes or until cooked through.

You can't clean up the world with soft soap – it takes grit.

JULY 25

BUTTERMILK SHAKE

1 c. buttermilk
2 T. honey
1 T. lemonade concentrate

Place all ingredients in a blender and process until smooth.

You can't keep trouble from coming – but you don't have to offer it a comfortable chair to sit in.

JUNE 9

TOMATO RELISH

2 tomatoes, chopped
1 onion, chopped
1 tsp. ground cumin
1/4 c. olive oil
Salt and pepper

Combine all ingredients together. Chill and serve.

*The best way to enjoy summer is to turn the
air-conditioner on and the TV set off.*

JULY 24

CARAMEL ORANGES

2 seedless oranges, peeled and sliced
1/4 c. amber or caramel sauce

Top oranges with caramel sauce. Let oranges sit for an hour before serving.

The best way to save daylight is to use it.

JUNE 10

APPLE ICED TEA

1 c. prepared ice tea
1 c. apple juice

Combine tea and apple juice. Pour over ice in a tall glass and sweeten to taste.

Do you realize that it only took six days to create the entire world? It just goes to show you what can be done if you don't take coffee breaks.

JULY 23

PEAS IN A POD

1 carton garden vegetable cream cheese
Fresh sweet pea pods
Frozen green peas, thawed

Split open the seam of the pea pod with a sharp knife. Open the pea pod and stuff with cream cheese. Place three peas on the cheese and serve.

*Some people eat so fast they have racing stripes
on their knives and forks.*

JUNE 11

Chocolate Fruit Drop

1/2 c. chocolate chips, melted
1 c. raspberries, or favorite fruit
1/4 c. chopped nuts

Drop spoonfuls of melted chocolate on wax paper and top each drop with fruit and nuts. Place in refrigerator until set. Peel the chocolate drops off wax paper and serve.

There is nothing more strenuous than having to push the thought of chocolate to the back of the mind.

JULY 22

Chocolate Marshmallow Shake

1 c. vanilla ice cream
2 T. milk
2 T. chocolate syrup
2 T. marshmallow cream

Combine all ingredients in a blender and process until smooth.

*The simplest things are often hardest to grasp –
like soap in a bath.*

JUNE 12

Pesto Pizza

1/2 c. pesto
1 tomato, thinly sliced
1/2 c. mozzarella cheese
1 prepared pizza crust

Top baked pizza crust with pesto. Top with tomato and grated cheese.
Return to the oven at 350° just until cheese is melted.

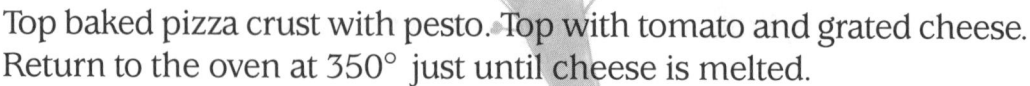

*Nothing is so strong as gentleness, nothing so gentle
as real strength.*

JULY 21

STRAWBERRY VINEGAR

4 c. sliced fresh strawberries
1 c. white wine vinegar
2 tsp. sugar

Combine all ingredients and let stand at room temperature for 24 hours. Strain the vinegar through a coffee filter into a bottle and seal.

*An open mind leaves a chance for someone
to drop a worthwhile thought in it.*

JUNE 13

HERB PESTO

2 c. fresh basil
1/2 c. olive oil
2 cloves garlic, crushed
2 T. walnuts
1/2 c. parmesan cheese, grated

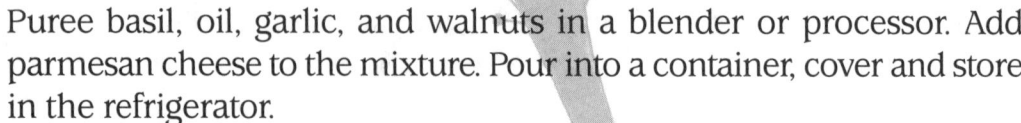

Puree basil, oil, garlic, and walnuts in a blender or processor. Add parmesan cheese to the mixture. Pour into a container, cover and store in the refrigerator.

Memory is what a motorist uses to almost find the right way.

JULY 20

FRUITED AVOCADO

1 avocado, halved
1 c. mixed fruit of choice, chopped
2 T. honey
1 T. strawberry vinegar

Combine honey and vinegar with fruit and mound into the two halves of the avocado.

Food is an important part of a balanced diet.

JUNE 14

"Watermelon" Mold

1 pint lime sherbet, slightly softened
1 pint pineapple sherbet, slightly softened

1 pint raspberry sherbet, slightly softened
2 T. mini chocolate chips

Line a 1 quart bowl with saran wrap. Spoon the lime sherbet evenly around the inner surface of the bowl. Place in freezer until hardened. Then spoon the pineapple sherbet over the lime and place back into freezer. Mix the raspberry sherbet and the chips and fill the center of the bowl, then place in freezer until solid. To unmold, turn contents of bowl onto plate and remove saran wrap. Slice the "watermelon" and serve.

A laugh is a smile that burst.

JULY 19

HAM FINGERS

8 oz. ham
1/2 c. sour cream
1 T. Dijon mustard

Cut the ham into 2 inch strips. Combine sour cream and mustard. Dip ham in mustard and serve.

Correcting faults is like tying a necktie; we can do it easier on ourselves than on anybody else.

JUNE 15

FRUIT DIP

1 c. sour cream
1/4 c. brown sugar

Mix ingredients and serve with fruit for dipping.

*There are those who believe they can push themselves
forward by constantly patting themselves on the back.*

JULY 18

Piña Colada French Toast

2 eggs, beaten
4 slices French bread
1 c. shredded coconut
1 T. butter

Dip bread in beaten egg and then in coconut. Fry in a pan with melted butter until golden on both sides. Serve with pineapple syrup.

The purpose of life is a life of purpose.

JUNE 16

BROWNIE PIZZA

1 package brownie mix
8 oz. package cream
   cheese, softened

1/4 c. sugar
Sliced strawberries
1/2 c. chocolate, melted

Prepare the brownie mix according to instructions. Spread dough onto a greased 12 inch pizza pan and bake according to directions. After crust has cooled top with a mixture of cream cheese and sugar. Top with strawberries and drizzle with chocolate and serve.

*It is a serious drought when washing your car
won't produce rain.*

JULY 17

Pineapple Syrup

1 small can crushed pineapple, drained
1/3 c. maple syrup

Combine in small saucepan and warm. Serve with French toast.

*Americans are getting into shape. Twenty years ago
it took two adults to carry fifty dollars' worth of groceries.
Today a child can do it.*

JUNE 17

FRUIT AND PASTA

1 c. mixed fresh fruit, diced
2 c. cooked spiral noodles
1/2 c. vanilla yogurt
Dash of cinnamon

Toss all ingredients together and serve.

*Ever notice how many people eat with their fingers and talk
with their fork?*

JULY 16

TWICE DIPPED STRAWBERRIES

1 pint strawberries, rinsed and dried
1/2 c. dark chocolate chips, melted
1/2 c. white chocolate chips, melted

Hand dip the strawberries first in the dark chocolate. Place on wax paper in the refrigerator until firm. Then dip the tip into the white chocolate and set on wax paper until firm.

Nothing spoils a good party like a genius.

JUNE 18

CHOCOLATE RASPBERRY PIE

Prepared chocolate cookie pie crust
1 quart raspberry ice cream or sherbet, slightly softened
1 quart vanilla ice cream, slightly softened
1 c. fudge sauce

Spoon vanilla ice cream into the cookie crust. Top with the fudge and refrigerate until firm. Spoon raspberry ice cream on the top and place into freezer until firm.

Life is like playing a violin solo in public and learning the instrument as you go on.

JULY 15

HERB TRIANGLES

3 T. green onions, finely chopped
1/2 c. mixed herbs, finely chopped
10 slices thin white bread, crusts removed
1/2 c. unsalted butter, softened

Combine green onions and herbs. Butter one side of bread and press into herbs. Butter the other side and press into herbs. Cut into triangles and serve.

*What is a weed? A plant whose virtues
have not yet been discovered.*

JUNE 19

MILWAUKEE BRATS

6 fresh brats
1 bottle of beer
1 c. sauerkraut
6 buns

Simmer brats in beer for about 20 minutes. Continue cooking brats on grill until brown. Remove cooked brats and place in buns and top with sauerkraut.

Why is it the neighbor's barbecue always smells better than ours tastes?

JULY 14

MANDARIN DESSERT

1 pint of orange sherbet
1 can mandarin oranges, drained

Scoop the sherbet into bowls and top with mandarin orange.

After dinner, some families suffer from dish-temper.

JUNE 20

GRILLED PINEAPPLE

4 pineapple rings
4 Tbls. brown sugar

Place pineapple on foil on the grill. Top with brown sugar. Grill until sugar is melted and pineapple is heated through.

A real friend is one who will visit you on a hot day even if you don't have air-conditioning.

JULY 13

Sweet Won Ton Bows

1 pkg. Won ton wrappers
2 c. oil
Powdered sugar

Pinch won ton wrappers together in the middle to form a bow. Fry in hot oil until golden. Drain on paper toweling and sprinkle with powdered sugar. Serve with Mandarin Dessert.

Those who always aim for perfection will soon discover that it is a moving target.

JUNE 21

DINOSANDWICH

2 dinosaur graham cookies
2 T. whipped topping
1 T. mini chocolate chips

Spread one cookie with whipped topping and sprinkle with chocolate chips. Top with remaining cookie.

Dirt is not really dirt – only something in the wrong place.

JULY 12

CHOCOLATE CREAM CHEESE

8 oz. cream cheese, softened
1/4 c. cream
4 T. powdered sugar
3 oz. chocolate, melted

Beat the cream cheese with the cream and powdered sugar. Add melted chocolate and continue to beat until smooth. Chill until ready to serve. Serve with ginger snaps and fruit.

The waist is a terrible thing to mind.

JUNE 22

MELON MIX

1 cantaloupe
1 honeydew
1 tsp. lemon juice
2 T. honey

Cut and seed each melon. Cut into 1 inch cubes or balls with melon baller. Toss with honey and lemon and serve.

The toughest part of dieting isn't watching what you eat, it's watching what your friends eat.

JULY 11

SUMMER PUDDING

3 c. raspberry sauce
1 loaf thin sliced bakery style white bread

Line a two quart bowl with saran wrap and spoon 1/2 the berry sauce in the bottom. Cut the crusts off the bread and place the slices overlapping around the edge. Add more berry sauce and more bread until the mixture is used up. Cover with saran wrap and weight it down with a plate. Refrigerate overnight. Unmold and serve.

Glutton: A person who takes the piece of pie you wanted.

JUNE 23

PEACH COBBLER

1 tube refrigerated biscuit dough
1 can peach pie filling
2 T. butter
2 T. sugar

Place 1/4 c. pie filling in small custard cup. Flatten biscuit slightly and place on top of filling. Brush with butter and sprinkle with sugar. Bake according to instructions on biscuit can.

Evening is that period of time when people do the craziest things to keep from going to bed.

JULY 10

SPINACH STUFFED MUSHROOMS

12 oz. mushrooms, cleaned
1 package Stouffer® Spinach Soufflé, thawed

Remove stems from the mushrooms. Fill cavities with spoonfuls of spinach soufflé. Place on pan and cook for 15 minutes in a 350° oven.

Happiness is good health and a bad memory.

JUNE 24

WHITE BEAN DIP

1 can white beans, drained
2 green onions, chopped
2 T. Lemon juice
2 T. parsley, chopped
6 T. olive oil

Place all ingredients in a blender and process until smooth. Salt and pepper to taste. Serve with vegetables.

Celery is a vegetable that should be seen and not heard.

JULY 9

PEPPERONI BREAD

1 loaf frozen bread dough, thawed
3 oz. pepperoni
1 c. mozzarella cheese, grated

Roll out the dough into a 12 by 8 inch rectangle. Place the pepperoni over the dough and top with grated cheese. Roll up bread jelly roll fashion. Place on pan seam side down. Let rise 1/2 hour, then bake in a 350° oven for 25 minutes.

*The hardest thing to learn is which bridge to burn
and which bridge to cross.*

JUNE 25

WATERMELON SLUSH

2 c. watermelon, seeded, peeled and diced
1/2 c. apple juice
1 T. lemon juice

Place watermelon on a wax paper covered cookie sheet and freeze.
Place frozen melon, apple juice, and lemon juice in the blender. Process
until slush. Pour into two glasses and serve.

*Watermelon is the only fruit you can eat, drink,
and wash your face in.*

JULY 8

SUMMER FRUIT TREE

Styrofoam cone
Green or plain foil
Toothpicks
Assorted fruit

Wrap styrofoam with foil. Stick fruit on one end of the toothpick and stick the other in the tree. Pluck fruit from tree and serve with chocolate cream cheese.

Grapefruit – the most frequently used eyewash.

JUNE 26

BLUE CHEESE LOAF

1/2 c. blue cheese, crumbled
1/2 c. butter, room temperature
1 loaf Italian bread

Make slices in the loaf, 1/2 inch apart and 3/4 of the way down. Keep the loaf together at the bottom. Combine the butter and blue cheese and spread between slices. Wrap loaf in foil and heat in a 350° oven for about 20 minutes.

Ideas are funny – they don't work unless you do.

JULY 7

Taco Pizza

1 flour tortilla
1/4 c. pepper cheese, grated
2 T. sliced black olives
2 T. whole kernel corn

Brush tortilla with water and heat in a 350° oven for 3 minutes. Top with cheese, olives, and corn. Return to the oven until heated through and the cheese is melted.

If you want to keep your dishes clean, eat out of the pans.

JUNE 27

BLUSHING SANDWICH

2 slices white bread
1 T. strawberry cream cheese
1 slice smoked chicken

Spread one slice of bread with the cream cheese and place chicken and the other slice of bread on top.

A success is a failure with a fresh coat of paint.

JULY 6

Banana Pops

1 large banana, cut in half
1/4 c. chocolate, melted
1/4 c. peanuts, chopped
2 popsicle sticks

Place popsicle stick in each banana half. Dip each in the chocolate and roll in peanuts. Place in freezer until frozen.

Life is too short to eat brown bananas.

JUNE 28

Muffin Surprise

1 muffin, your favorite flavor
2 T. whipped topping

Cut top off muffin and scoop out the center. Mix the crumbled center and whipped topping. Spoon the mixture into muffin center and replace top.

Working in the kitchen is like having a baby – there are just some things you have to do by yourself.

JULY 5

STUFFED CHERRY TOMATO

1 can shrimp, drained and rinsed
2 T. mayonnaise
1 T. capers, chopped
Cherry tomatoes

Combine shrimp, mayonnaise and capers. Cut top off cherry tomato and scoop out seeds with a melon baller. Stuff with shrimp mixture.

There's a new gardening magazine out –
it's called Weeder's Digest.

JUNE 29

ALL AMERICAN PIE

7 c. fresh fruit – strawberries, blueberries and sliced banana
1 ready made cookie crust
1/2 c. sugar
2 T. cornstarch
1/2 c. lemonade

Mix cornstarch and sugar in a saucepan. Add lemonade and bring to boil, stirring until thickened. Cool glaze for 10 minutes. Pour over fruit and toss gently. Pour into pie shell and chill.

America is still the land of opportunity – where else could you earn enough to owe so much?

JULY 4

ICE CREAM PUNCH

1 pint orange vanilla swirl ice cream
2 c. orange juice
1 large bottle ginger ale

Spoon the ice cream into a punch bowl. Add the orange juice and stir to blend. Add the ginger ale and serve.

If laughter really were the best medicine, hospitals would have found a way to charge us for it long ago.

JUNE 30

RED, WHITE AND BLUE SALSA

1 c. fresh sliced strawberries
1/2 c. blueberries
1/4 c. pecans, chopped
2 T. strawberry or cider vinegar
2 T. brown sugar
1 T. vegetable oil

Whisk together vinegar, sugar and oil. Pour over a mixture of berries and pecans. Serve with grilled meat.

To make the sun shine – just call off the picnic.

JULY 3

Fish Fry Sandwich

1 frozen breaded fish fillet
2 slices rye bread
1/4 c. prepared coleslaw

Bake fillet according to directions. Place fish on rye bread and top with coleslaw and rye bread.

A fish is an animal that grows fastest between the time it is caught and the time the fisherman describes it to his friends.

JULY 1

FRESH TOMATO JUICE

1 ripe tomato
Salt and pepper to taste
2 ice cubes

Place ice and tomato in blender and process until smooth. Pour into glass and season to taste.

Summer is the time when you don't want to do all those things you've been wanting to do all winter.

JULY 2

BEVERAGES

BEVERAGES

BREADS AND SANDWICHES

BREADS AND SANDWICHES

CAKES AND PIES

CAKES AND PIES

CANDY/CONFECTIONS

CANDY/CONFECTIONS

COOKIES/BARS

DESSERTS

EGGS

FRUIT

FRUIT

MEAT AND FISH

PASTA/PIZZA

PASTRY

SAUCES, SPREADS & DIPS

SAUCES, SPREADS & DIPS

VEGETABLES

MISCELLANEOUS